Retrospectives

A Scrum Master's Guide

Daria Bagina

SCRU**M**ASTERED

First Edition

Table of Contents

Preface

I remember my very first real retrospective session with a new team. I was still new to the Scrum Master role and never really facilitated or led a similar event ever before, so I was quite nervous about running it successfully.

I spent at least two days preparing for it, researching the web, reading books and articles. Each article had a great selection of activities to try in a retrospective, but no real instructions I could follow. Each activity had to be mixed-and-matched with another one to build a perfect retrospective.

As a person obsessed with organizing everything, I decided to write my own step-by-step guide for my first retrospective session right in my notebook: I needed a handy tool to refer to during the facilitation to keep on track. The other thing I focused on was specific words I wanted to say to help the team understand - I didn't want to mumble nonsense after all.

When I finally got to the retrospective, I was very unsure of how successful my facilitation is going to be as I have written it myself without anyone's help. It was only normal for me to be skeptical about the guide I have written since I was only starting my journey as a Scrum Master.

At the end of the next sprint, I had to go through the exercise again to prepare a new retrospective session to keep the team engaged. A lot of time was spent on preparation, some time spent on worrying about the success of the session.

As I was facilitating more retrospectives I started to collect more step-by-step instructions for different types of techniques. It was my personal go-to resource for getting ready for each session. I realized that I must be just one of many Scrum Masters looking for similar tools to help them get more productive facilitation.

That is where the idea for this book came from. I wanted to build a guide that can be used by a Scrum Master with any level of experience to easily facilitate successful retrospective sessions and keep their teams engaged; not just a book as a collection of ideas, but an actual tool that can be added to a Scrum Master's toolbox to take away the stress and allow you to focus on facilitation.

1

RETROSPECTIVE BASICS

You might already know what a retrospective is and why it is important, or maybe you just quickly read about it in the Scrum Guide or heard about it in your Scrum certification training. You might have picked up this book by curiosity, or even mistake.

Whatever the situation is, let's have a quick recap of what a retrospective is and why you would want to run it at the end of every sprint or iteration.

Let us look at the Agile Manifesto that started it all. One of the twelve principles technically describes retrospectives in a nutshell:

"At regular intervals, the team reflects on how to become more effective, then tunes and adjusts its behaviour accordingly."

This is the essential truth. To be Agile or to become more Agile you should be striving to continuously improve, meaning review your ways of working and adapt them to the changing environment or better them to allow the team to become happier and more effective.

When we look at the Scrum Guide it becomes clear that the purpose of a retrospective is to give teams a formal opportunity to inspect their processes and current situation and create a plan for improvements.

At this point, you might be thinking that a retrospective sounds quite similar to a post-mortem that is widely used in traditional project management. However, it seems that way only on the surface.

A team retrospective is focused on finding solutions that can be implemented immediately in the next iterations by the team itself. Retrospectives happen all the way throughout the project (or better:

product development) allowing to make adjustments on the go and see the results of the experiments.

Post-mortems on the other hand often focus on things that had already happened and can no longer be changed. Usually, it is too late to act and what the teams are trying to do it to avoid running into the same mistake again in the next project. Another big difference is that solutions identified are usually distributed across different teams and even departments, which takes away control from the people most impacted by the challenges these solutions are trying to address. The solutions usually are planned for in advance and are rarely changed along the way when the new information is discovered.

A retrospective stays internal to the group in question and aims at empowering this group to experiment and change in the spirit of continuous improvement.

A retrospective is by the team and for the team. Always remember this important premise when you run your session.

I would say that this summarizes pretty much everything you need to know about a retrospective and its importance in an Agile environment. Now let us think about the more practical side of things.

A CURIOUS CASE OF BORING RETROSPECTIVES

Let's get this one clear - there is no "one fits all" solution. It just doesn't exist. There is also no perfect Scrum approach. What works the best, and has been proven in real life by numerous agile practitioners, is a situational approach. Meaning, figure out what's going on and use tools that will help you in that particular situation.

What does it have to do with retrospectives?

We all know how important retrospectives are in any Agile process (as we just covered it in the previous section). They allow us to inspect and adapt, hence improve, every Sprint.

Now, imagine going to a retrospective every two weeks (which is a common sprint length these days) and having to answer the same old questions

"What went well?" and "What can be improved?"

"What went well?" and "What can be improved?"...

"What went well?" and "What can be improved?"...

"What went well?" and "What..."

You got the picture.

It's possible that your retrospectives became stale after a while if you always use the same technique and you always ask the same questions. Your teams are getting bored, you are getting bored, and the action items start to sound more and more like a jammed record.

That is why I believe that using different retrospective techniques is essential to becoming more Agile by improving every sprint. And here is why.

- **Increased engagement.** You simply can't keep doing the same thing over and over again expecting people to stay interested. That is why providing your teams with a choice of techniques will help them get engaged in each retrospective you hold. It will almost turn it into a game.

- **Variety of results.** Different techniques provide you with an opportunity to look at the same problems from different angles which it turn might bring you new ideas of how to solve those problems. What I also found interesting, that new techniques help you uncover some of the hidden issues that no one on the team ever mentioned before.

- **Personalized analysis.** With a variety of techniques to use, you can easily direct your team at looking at the issues that are more relevant to them. If there's a specific problem you would like to solve, you can choose the best technique to talk about it.

- **Better statistics.** Once you set up a set of techniques, you can finally start collecting some feedback about them. Simple questions about how the team liked a certain technique will go a long way in perfecting your Scrum Master Toolbox.

- **Fun.** As simple as that. Especially if you have multiple teams to work with, doing the same thing every Retrospective will quickly become tedious. This will not only be more fun for your teams, but for you as well.

These five reasons are taken from an article I have written back in 2017 when I was really getting into this topic.

Agile retrospectives is a popular topic. There are tons of books (namely, Agile Retrospectives by Esther Derby, Diana Larsen and Ken Schwaber, which I highly recommend) and free resources about this topic and most of them are practical. However, so far I have not seen one that gives you a step-by-step guide on how to run a session from start to finish with cues on what to say.

This book is exactly what others are not - a step-by-step guide that you can put into your pocket and follow during your retrospective.

Especially since Scrum Master days can get pretty busy and when it's time for a retrospective you might not be ready with something new, or you might not be sure which technique to use to help you approach a specific situation.

That is where this book comes in!

Over the past years, I've been collecting retrospective techniques into a knowledge base and easy-to-use retrospective Poker cards to help me facilitate these events more efficiently.

In this book, I will share detailed instructions to each technique to run a retrospective from start to finish and will explain how to use retrospective Poker cards with your teams to make your sprint sessions more engaging.

Be assured that the techniques in this book were meticulously developed based on real-life experiences with the actual teams I worked with, therefore, the information here is on point.

I have also included helpful scripts you can use to explain different steps to your teams with ease.

I believe this can become your go-to tool to run awesome retrospectives. Just having a handy tool with you at all times is all that matters. Moreover, you can pass it on to your fellow Scrum Masters who are just starting out with a new team or even give it to your team members while you are on vacation, to ensure they run productive retrospectives even when you are not around.

THE DO'S AND DONT'S OF RETROSPECTIVES

Each retrospective technique requires active facilitation by a Scrum Master or an agile practitioner. The techniques work best with the whole team being co-located and attending it in person. Though online tools can be used for some of the techniques, not all of them can be performed using them.

If you are facilitating these retrospectives in person with your team, prepare the usual materials for your session:

- A whiteboard or a flipchart, obviously.
- Whiteboard (dry-erase) markers for the facilitator. You may also use sharpies, but know, that you will have a hard time wiping them off the board.
- Sticky notes, enough to distribute among the team members.
- Sharpies or pens, 1 per team member. I would recommend sharpies, though, as you can see the writing from a distance.

Steps to run any retrospective

Though each technique in this book is unique and will require a certain set of steps to be successfully facilitated, there is a basic structure that almost any technique will follow. As you go through the instructions for each technique, keep this structure in mind. This structure also aligns with what Esther Derby, Diana Larsen and Ken Schwaber described in their book Agile retrospectives (Agile Retrospectives: Making Good Teams Great, 2006).

1. **Prepare any necessary drawings and graphs** before the team arrives.

2. **Follow up on the action items from the previous retrospective.** This is an important step to hold the team accountable for what they agreed upon together. This step is often skipped, but I feel it is the most important one to start the retrospective in the right way - it reminds everyone that this is a working session with a specific goal, not just a talking meeting.

3. **Present the technique by going over the main topic of the discussion** or explaining the metaphor you are giving. This will set the stage for the rest of the session.

4. **Gather ideas from the team according to the technique**. You will need to ask different questions for every technique. There are many different ways to gather ideas and each can be used in a variety of situations. However, for certain techniques, I have added a different way to gather ideas as I felt that it helps align the whole session better.

5. **Run the session** according to the technique instructions.

6. **Define solutions of action items the team would like to focus on in the next sprint**. The goal of any retrospective is to help teams continuously improve. It means that at the end of each session the team should come up with action items and experiments they want to try the next sprint. Don't turn your retrospectives into a complaint session - focus on solving the issues at hand.

7. **Ask for volunteers to drive the action items**. Remind the team that if an action item has no owner, it will most likely is not getting done. It doesn't mean that the person driving the action is the only one responsible for its completion, it is just a person who should be following up on this action with the team and making sure that the team hold each other accountable for it. The real owner of each action is the whole team. Here are some speaking cues you can use:

> *"An unassigned action item will not get done. Every action needs an owner - a person to drive it and to remind the team that we agreed to do it. This person will only be the driver of the action, the responsibility for completing that action still lies on the whole team. Let's make sure each action has a driver."*

> *"Remember that each action item needs to have a driver in order to get to completion. It will still be the team's responsibility to see these tasks to completion. We should identify a driver for each task we decide to take into the next sprint. Who would like to volunteer?"*

> *"Improvement is something we are responsible for, therefore, we need to make sure that the action items we have come up with are followed up on by someone from the team. What actions should we take into our next sprint and who would like to drive them?"*

> *"There are a lot of good ideas listed after our discussion. We will not be able to focus on all of them. Let's decide what is doable next sprint and think who can drive each action. If we are not sure where to start on a certain action, we can meet during the sprint to discuss our plan or decide to do just a small portion of a bigger improvement initiative."*

> *"It is time to start thinking about the ways we can improve it. What would be the smallest thing we can change in the way we work, to positively impact this area? What can be done right away, for example, next sprint? Is there a bigger initiative that we can start? Do we need help from our management teams or other teams who work with us? How can we involve them?"*

8. **Close the session by summing up what has been identified** and agreed upon as well as by thanking the team for participating.

Solutions should be the focus of any retrospective. Unfortunately, there are some challenges that often appear in relation to action items. A lot of the times because of these challenges everyone seems to forget why they started to do retrospectives in the first place. This is when a retrospectives start to lose their meaning and the team becomes more reluctant to have any more of these "useless meetings".

Don't let your retrospectives turn into a useless meeting.

Let us review some of the challenges related to action items that often prevent retrospectives from being useful and let us go over potential solutions that you can easily implement.

Too many action items

Often teams get carried away by trying to solve every single issue they are facing right now. If your list of action items becomes too long by the end of the retrospective (6+ items), conduct a dot voting exercise to choose the most important ones. It will bring the focus back to the actual tangible results.

Not enough action items

Sometimes the brainstorming is just not going the way it was planned. In this case, encourage the team to come up with one single action item that will make their lives a bit easier next sprint. It will remove the pressure of coming up with plenty of ideas.

Vague action items

Nothing discourages continuous improvement as unclear goals. If the action items are not actionable or don't yield clear results, ask the team if this is even relevant. If yes, ask them to rephrase it into something more specific.

Once you have the action items list, the last important thing to do is to assign people to drive these activities. Each item should have an owner, though, you would want the team to volunteer themselves.

To ease the decision here, remind the team that the driver is not necessarily the person to complete the item, but the person to follow up on it and remind the team about it if needed.

Retrospectives can be tough for a number of reasons, especially, if you are new to the team or you have not run a lot of retrospectives yet. There are some common challenges that can happen during the session. A lot of them can be addressed with the simple techniques listed below. Always keep these techniques in mind as they can be useful in many situations.

Talking stick

In a case where most ideas come from a single person in your sessions, or you have some quiet team members who never talk, you can use a talking stick to help the situation. For this, choose any object that will represent the talking stick, for example, a whiteboard marker. Explain to the team, that only the person who has the talking stick is allowed to speak and you, the facilitator, has the right to reclaim the talking stick at any time. However, if the talking stick has been passed to you, you need to say at least something: "I pass" is not an option here.

Once you start the discussion during the session, give the talking stick to someone randomly and look for clues of other team members wanting to talk. You can use this together with the timer technique.

Dot voting

As mentioned above, sometimes when you have too many items to discuss and not enough time, you need to choose the most important ones to focus on.

Give everyone at least 3 votes or 3 dots (that is where the name is coming from). Depending on the number of people and notes, you might want to increase the number of votes everyone has. Usually, it's about 20% of the number of notes.

Ask each person to put their dots on sticky notes they would like to discuss. They can put all dots on one note or spread them among several notes. This techniques is used for physical sticky notes, but some other tools like funretro.io have the voting system integrated with it as well.

Timer

If you are like me and sometimes find yourself running your retrospective for too long, try the timer technique. Define a timer for one discussion topic or question, usually 5 minutes, and explain the rules to the team. When the time is up, everyone should vote on whether they want to continue the discussion on the same topic or not. If yes, send another timer for this topic and finish the discussion on this topic it the time is up again.

MODIFY EVERYTHING

Sometimes you would want to use different techniques to increase the idea flow of the team. In this case, feel free to change up almost any retrospective technique by changing brainstorming activities.

Brainstorming

Instead of asking the team to write their ideas on sticky notes, you can try to bring more engagement into the exercise in a different way.

Circle Around

Give the team a couple of minutes to think about the questions related to the introduced retrospective technique. Go around the table asking each team member to give you one single idea to write on the board. Depending on the size of the team, go around from two to four times.

Divide and Conquer

Divide categories in the technique between the team members and ask each of them to only write ideas related to the category they cover but to write as much as possible.

Bullet List

Distribute blank pieces of paper around the room. Ask each team member to write one sentence and mark which category it relates to depending on the technique you use. Then ask everyone to rotate the papers around the table clockwise. Now the next team member needs to write a follow-up sentence to what was written before. Rotate again. Continue until the paper returns to the initial writer.

Group Together

This could work especially well if you have a bigger team. Ask everyone to pair up for the brainstorming exercise with the person next to them. They need to finish the exercise by quickly deciding what sticky notes to write.

Shout It Out

When your brainstorming exercise becomes slow and unproductive, try out this activity that can sparkle more ideas. Ask each person to write their idea on a sticky and as soon as they are done writing say the idea out loud and put it in the center of the table. It might be disrupted at the beginning but will make the whole brainstorming activity more effective. Remember to remind the team that they should not comment on the ideas presented at this stage - the point of this is to generate as many ideas as possible, the sorting exercise will happen later.

Voting

Voting on ideas is going to be an important part of your retrospective. To be able to get to a consensus within your timebox you will need to use some common techniques. Here are a couple of different voting ideas that you can try.

Fist of five

This is a commonly known technique that is used in the Agile world.

Each person can evaluate each idea by showing 1 to 5 fingers on their hand. '5' would represent that the idea is great and the team member really thinks it's worth the team's time. '1' would represent the opposite - this idea is not something the team should spend time on. It will allow for a more granular analysis of options at hand.

Yes-No-Whatever

This technique is usually used in Lean Coffee but can be a great voting tool in any situation.

Each team member needs to vote on an idea by showing a thumbs-up - "this is a great idea, we should do it"; a thumbs-down - "enough, let's move on" or thumbs sideways - "I'll support any group decision".

It is very easy to understand how much support a certain topic has.

ENGAGING YOUR TEAM IN ADVANCE

Successful retrospective does not happen just during the session itself. If your team is dreading going to the room because they do not know what to expect, it can be a challenge to get them engaged when the session has started already.

You can get much better results if you include your team in retrospective discussions in advance if you get them excited and looking forward to the session - it is practically half of your success already.

If you can do it, engage your team in the retrospective even before they walk into the room.

I am extremely happy to finally be able to talk about retrospective Poker - something that I developed specifically for the reasons described above.

The idea about this came during a brainstorming session with my colleague Scrum Masters. Our goal was to find a way to easily choose retrospective techniques each sprint as well as engage teams into the process.

After going through some wild but very fun ideas we finally ended up on cards - though, it didn't seem like a very fun thing, it turned out to be the perfect medium for doing what we intended it to do.

After using the cards we designed in a matter of a couple of days with the teams, I believed in their value even more. Now fast-forward a year >>>

Working on perfecting the cards, expanding and refining the list of techniques it can be used with, creating beautiful design resulted in the completely new and unique set of Retrospective Poker cards that go along the book you are reading right now.

The Retrospective Poker cards are now available for purchase on my website: http://www.scrummastered.com/buy-retrospective-poker

Information on the cards

Each card contains the name of the technique and a brief explanation. In a separate line, you will find what the technique focuses on - it will allow you to decide which situation is the most appropriate for this retrospective type.

The card also contains information about the typical duration and difficulty of facilitation. The duration usually depends on how chatty your team is, but this can still give you a clue on how much time you might need. Difficulty mostly relates to how hard it is to facilitate productive discussions as some techniques are more prone to focus on action items while others are more conversation based.

Using the cards as a game

With the use of the Retrospective Poker cards you will be able to look through available retrospective techniques and choose the one that works best for you in the current situation: whether what area you would like the team to focus on, how prepared you are for the facilitation or how much time you have.

The other way to use the cards is to give them to your team to choose. First of all, it will allow them to start discussions among themselves to define what they want to focus on as a team. Secondly, they will get into the retrospective session even before it starts - it does become kind of a game for the team.

If the decision seems to be too difficult, the team can still be involved in the game. Shuffle the cards and ask the team to nominate one team member to blindly choose a card from the deck. Voila!

The best part, you can arrange the deck the way you want before giving it to the team, for example, by removing techniques you don't want to focus on that time.

Using the cards as a guide

You can also use the cards during your retrospective session to guide you.

While the cards themselves do not provide you detailed steps, if you have already run the technique once, you will easily remember what it was about and how to run it again by simply looking at the statements on the cards.

Less preparation, better facilitation!

To order the cards, head to *http://www.scrummastered.com/buy-retrospective-poker*

2

ADAPTING YOUR APPROACH

When you start working with a team, as a Scrum Master you would first want to take enough time to observe them. You would want to understand the way the team works and makes decisions, where they are coming from.

While the act of having a retrospective and specific outcomes (a.k.a. action items) is quite prescribed, it is in your power as a Scrum Master to find the best approach that will work best for your team and for a specific situation.

As you spend more time with your team and observe them, you will learn more about how they operate. This is essential in deciding how to run your retrospectives.

The better you know your team and different personalities your team members have, the better the approach you will be able to take.

This book contains twenty different retrospective techniques and each one of them can be used with success in different situations - you are the best judge of what those situations are. However, it does not mean I am going to leave you without guidance.

Each technique contains details about when is the best time and situation to apply this retrospective. As you observe the team and the sprint, you will be able to understand what is happening and how a specific technique can bring the most productive discussions.

As you run more retrospectives you will see that the same techniques can bring different results depending on the team. Don't give up if a technique did not work out well. Keep going to find the best approach for your team.

HOW TO READ THIS BOOK

Very important note right here, so read carefully.

This book was never intended as a cover-to-cover type of reading. This book is a toolbox full of different tools that you can use in your retrospective events - you are not supposed to take out all the tools at once and start using them all right away.

Imagine that you are building a house (like building a new strong Agile team). You are not picking up your paintbrush and start colouring the ground if you don't have a foundation yet - you might want to pick up a shovel first.

Therefore, the best way to read the book is to find the tool you need right now. Decide what you are trying to achieve and look at the techniques at your disposal - the next short chapter describes how they are organized in the book. Then read the brief descriptions of each technique you feel can work for you and choose one that makes the most sense.

Once you have chosen the technique to run in your next retrospective, read the rest of the instructions and get ready to facilitate an amazing session.

Each technique will have a title page that will contain all the necessary information for you to run the technique. You can easily print this one page for reference during the session without having to go through the whole list of instructions once you get familiar with the technique.

GETTING READY

When you prepare for your retrospective, you will most likely look into different options available to you in general as well as your level of comfort with the team and the technique you would like to run.

All techniques can be viewed from a set of factors that will help you identify which one to use and when. When you prepare for the retrospective think about these factors: your experience level, how mature the team is and how much time you want to spend.

Your experience with facilitation

When I was working on the book, I wanted to make sure that there are techniques for a variety of situations as well as experience levels of Scrum Masters. That is why techniques in this book have a different level of difficulty in terms of facilitation. As you grow in the role of a Scrum Master, you will learn how to facilitate difficult or long discussions.

If you are just starting out or new to your team, I would suggest starting with techniques at the beginning. As you build relationships with your team and become more used to running retrospectives, move to techniques further in the chapter.

Even if you are more experienced running retrospectives, you would want to look into techniques at the beginning of the list as they might be a good fit for a specific situation.

Team maturity

Any team is going through different stages of maturity that were described in Bruce Tuckman's Forming, Storming, Norming, and Performing model. If you have not heard about this model yet, let me save you some time now by giving you a brief explanation. Though, you should read up on it as it is a very commonly used model that will help you understand your team better.

As the team forms, it is going through some stages of becoming more mature as a team. When people are just assigned to working together, they are in the **forming** stage, trying to figure out their roles and responsibilities.

As they start to work more together, they pass into the **storming** stage where they don't know how to work together and often can have conflicts because their roles are not clearly identified.

As they start to form working agreements and figure out how to work together they pass into the **norming** stage.

When the team is finally gelled in and start working towards team goals together, they finally pass into the **performing** stage where they consistently deliver value.

Adjourning is the next stage of ultimate performance, but should be considered more as a direction for continuous improvement rather than a final goal.

In this book, these stages also represent how mature the team is in relation to Agile and Scrum. If the team is very new to this way of working, then they are in a forming state. If the team is quite advanced, then they are in the performing state.

That is why you will see that some techniques are better to run with mature teams as it will be easier to facilitate and will yield better results. However, you can still run them with any team if you feel it can bring good insights. As usual, as a Scrum Master, you know your team the best and will be able to choose a technique that would engage your team better.

Further in the book the symbols used for each stage will be as follows:

- Forming - ●○○○;
- Storming - ●●○○;
- Norming - ●●●○;
- Performing - ●●●●.

Available time

Another factor is the time you have for your retrospective. While you would usually schedule the same amount of time each sprint (you remember, it is done to reduce complexity?), you might want to allow time for a longer discussion for a particularly difficult sprint, for example, or, on the other hand, shorten your session to focus on a simpler topic.

Each technique has a different duration depending on the number of topics to discuss and their complexity. Obviously, it all depends on your facilitation and how much your team likes to talk. You can easily turn a short technique into a one and a half hour discussion, but in their core, certain techniques can be run faster than others based on my experience. Pay attention to how your team operates: if you know that your team likes to talk

Further in the book the symbols used for different lengths of sessions will be as follows:

- Short, can be done in 30 minutes - ●○○○○;
- Medium-short, can be done in around 45 minutes - ●●○○○;
- Medium, usually takes around an hour - ●●●○;
- Medium-long, a bit over an hour - ●●●●;
- Long, easily takes an hour and a half - ●●●●.

Here is a short overview of all the techniques in order in which they appear in the book:

Technique	Duration	Facilitation Difficulty	Team maturity
Lean Coffee	●○○○○	●○○	●○○○
Categories	●○○○○	●○○	●○○○
Starfish Diagram	●○○○○	●○○	●●●○
Sailboat	●●○○○	●○○	●○○○
Hot-Air Balloon	●●○○○	●○○	●○○○
Team Index	●●●○○	●○○	●●●○
People & Process	●●●○○	●○○	●○○○
Expectations	●○○○○	●●○	●○○○
Emotion Triggers	●●●●○	●●○	●●●○
Resolutions	●●●●●	●●○	●○○○
Success Stories	●●●○○	●●○	●●●○
Sprint Timeline	●●●●●	●●○	●●●○
Manifesto	●●●○○	●●○	●●○○
Three Circles	●●●○○	●●○	●●●○
Contradictions	●○○○○	●●○	●●●○
Learning Habits	●●●○○	●●●	●●●○
Experiments	●●●○○	●●●	●●●●
Anti-actions	●○○○○	●●●	●●●○
Question Time	●●●●●	●●●	●●●●
Value Tree	●●●●○	●●●	●●○○

Concept:

Lean Coffee started in Seattle in 2009 by Jim Benson and Jeremy Lightsmith.

INSTRUCTIONS

1. **Introduce the technique** by explaining that in this session the team has an opportunity to discuss any questions or topics they would like.

> *"Today I would like us to have a free forum discussion with each other using the Lean Coffee technique. It is up to you to define the topics. We are going to collect ideas from everyone in the room and then vote on which ones we would like to talk about."*

2. **Ask the team to write down what they would like to talk about in this session** - it can be an area of improvement, a suggestion, a particular challenge, a question, etc. One idea per sticky note.

> *"We will spend the next 5 minutes on generating ideas for our discussion. Pick up post-it notes and pens to write down your questions or topics you would like to discuss. One idea per post-it note, please. Let's strive to have at least one topic per person, and ideally two or three per person. While it is ok to have a couple of silly topics just for laughs, let's keep it professional and think about things that relate to our work, our processes and people we work with."*

3. **Collect the notes and put them up on the board** or ask the team members to do it. Either way, read each note out loud and make sure everyone understands what it is about.

> *"If everyone is ready, let's review what topics and questions we have. I will read each note out loud. If you are not sure what it refers to, please ask so that you understand all of the topics before we start voting."*

4. **Conduct dot voting exercise** giving everyone at least three votes.

> *"We only have so much time to have a discussion around the topics you have suggested, let's make sure we spend it on the most important ones. For this, we will do simple dot voting exercise. Grab a marker and get closer to the board. Each one of you has three votes, or three dots, that you can put on any topic on the board. You can put all three votes on one topic if you really want it to be at the top, or spread the votes in any way you want."*

5. **Rearrange the notes** by putting the notes with the most votes on top and with the least at the bottom.

> *"I am going to rearrange the notes on the board by putting the notes with the most votes at the top. We might not have enough time to cover all the topics. We will start with the topics with most votes and will progress towards the bottom."*

6. **Start with the note with the most votes.** Set a timer for five to eight minutes depending on how many topics you would like to cover. For each topic discuss the following:
  ○ What are the reasons for this topic/question to be upvoted?
  ○ What challenges are there for the team in relation to this topic?
  ○ What improvements can we make to address this topic?

> *"To make sure we have a productive discussion, we will limit the time we spend on each topic to 5 minutes. When the timer is up, we will vote on whether we want to continue to discuss the same topic or move on to the next one. We should have no more than two rounds on each topic. The goal for this discussion is to understand why this topic is important, whether it is a concern we want to solve and, if yes, find ways to solve it by suggestion action items we can work on next sprint."*

7. **After the time is up, ask the team if they would like to keep discussing this topic.** If yes, set up a timer for another 3-5 minutes. When the second timer is finished or the team decided to not continue the discussion, switch to the next most upvoted topic or question.

> *"Our time is up. Let's vote. Hold your thumb up if you want to continue the discussion of this topic, hold your thumb down if you want to move to the next topic or hold your thumb sideways if you will go with whatever the group decides."*

8. **Encourage discussing solutions and potential action items** the team would like to take in the next sprint. Ask for volunteers to drive the action items.

> *"The goal of each discussion is not just talking about the question or concern, but think about the ways we can improve the situation or something we can do to address the question. We do not try to solve or answer everything right here in this session, but understand what steps we can take in the upcoming sprint to help us."*

9. **Close the session** by thanking everyone for coming and for their great topics for discussion.

> *"In this session, we had a great opportunity to discuss a variety of topics, all of which were generated by the team which means they are important to you. I hope that you were able to raise and discuss your concerns. Now that we have a plan for the next sprint, I am confident we can address some of your questions. Thank you for your active participation in today's session."*

MODIFICATIONS

Directed discussion

If you would like to direct the discussion of your team towards discussing a particular area, set up a topic at the beginning and ask team members to come up with notes related to the topic only. That way the team still has the freedom to choose what to discuss, but the conversation will revolve around the specific area you chose.

FACILITATOR NOTES

It is ok to have a couple of silly questions or topics voted up. Once I and my team discussed the global warming problem in our retrospective. Don't prevent it if this happens as it will set up a positive mood in your session and will only make you lose 5 minutes in total. As long as you get the discussion back to the work-related topics, of course.

CATEGORIES

Define areas of improvement based on what worked or didn't work the last sprint.

DESCRIPTION

This technique is a baseline for many other ones, even described in this book. It looks at general categories of what went well and can be improved and has many modifications that make this technique easily reusable over and over again. This technique also generates high-level areas of improvement to focus on as team ideas are revealed.

All of the content is generated by the team and as a facilitator, you should guide them in grouping ideas together. It can be viewed as a more structured extension of the Lean Coffee technique. It will help focus the discussion on common topics brought up by the team.

Duration:	Facilitation difficulty:	Team maturity:
●○○○○	●○○	●○○○

WHITEBOARD SETUP

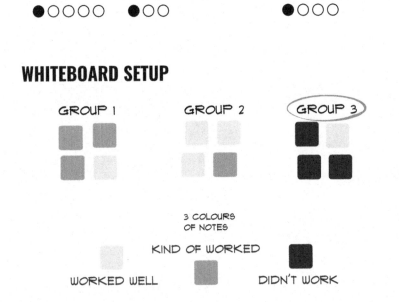

GROUP 1   GROUP 2   GROUP 3

3 COLOURS
OF NOTES

KIND OF WORKED

WORKED WELL   DIDN'T WORK

INSTRUCTIONS

1. **Introduce the three categories you would like the team to cover.** Talk about the fact that as a team you want to recognize our good work, as well as find areas of improvement in the future sprint.

> *"In today's retrospective, we will be able to see what areas need most of our attention. But to start off, we will look generally at what went well and didn't go well in the past sprint. This will allow us to recognize positive things that happened and identify what we can improve in the future."*

2. **Ask the team to think about what happened past sprint** and write it down on sticky notes:
  - What went well e.g. on green colour notes
  - What was ok, but could be improved e.g. on yellow colour notes
  - What did not work and hindered the team e.g. on red colour notes

> *"We have three colours of sticky notes: green ones for what worked well; yellow ones for what worked in a way but can be improved; and red ones for what didn't work and needs immediate attention. Think about different events or activities that happened in the past sprint and write down your ideas on the relevant coloured sticky note. One idea per sticky. Let's try to have at least one idea per person."*

3. **Collect the notes from everyone and start putting them on the whiteboard** one-by-one reading each out loud. As you add a note, ask the team if it is related to any previously placed notes and should be grouped together (regardless of the colour of the note). Your goal is to group as many notes as possible and end up with 5-6 groups.

> *"I will be reading the notes out loud and put them on the board. As I read the notes, let's think whether they are related to each other and can be grouped under one category. We will group the notes regardless of whether it is something that went well or not, as long as it belongs to the same category because we can have both positive and negative items related to the same general idea."*

4. **Review all notes and the groups identified** and ask the team to name it based on what notes are in it.

> *"To align our understanding, we should name each category. Let's go around the board and find an appropriate way of describing all items under that category."*

5. **Focus on the groups with the most negative notes** and start the discussion around what happened and what improvements can be implemented next sprint. Look both at positive and negative notes and see if anything can be derived from positive events to help with the challenges.

> *"While it would be great to discuss all categories in today's session, in the interest of time, we need to focus on the ones that require the most attention - the ones that have the most negative notes. These are the areas where we should be able to bring the most positive changes. We should look for patterns between different notes, whether they show something that worked well or not. As usual, our goal is to find ways to improve in this area, try something new next sprint."*

6. **Discuss as many groups as you have time for**. When the time is running out, ask the team which topic they would prefer to focus on.

> *"Unfortunately, we are running out of time. Let's make sure we discuss the most important topics before we go. Out of everything that is left on the board, what is the one topic you would definitely like to cover today? We should focus on that."*

7. **Ask for volunteers** to drive the action items.

8. **Close the session** by highlighting the areas that have been identified during the session and thanking everyone for participating.

> *"In this session, we were able to categorize the challenges and opportunities we are facing. It gave us a better understanding of the state of our work and processes from the positive and negative sides together. We should keep this in mind when working towards improving our ways of work in the next sprint."*

MODIFICATIONS

New categories

You can change this technique and its results by switching the categories to something a little bit different. For example:

- Mad, Sad, Glad
- Liked, Learned, Lacked

More categories

You can extend the number of initial categories to give the team more width to bring in new ideas. These categories can also bring a fun aspect to your retrospectives.

From the technique "Retro-wedding":

- *Something Old* – Positive feedback or constructive criticism on established practice.
- *Something New* – Positive feedback or constructive criticism on experiments in progress.
- *Something Borrowed* – Tools or ideas seen somewhere else that the team would like to try.
- *Something Blue* – Any blocker or source of sadness for the team.

From the video game "Sunless Skies":

- *Something ghastly* – Risks and uncertainties that may hinder the team's progress.
- *Something grave* – Challenges that have a negative impact on the team right now and should be resolved as soon as possible.
- *Something that glisters* – New ideas that seem promising.
- *Something to crave* – A reasonable wishlist, something that the team currently doesn't have but can work towards getting.

FACILITATOR NOTES

The team might be confused when you start grouping positive and negative notes together since they were grouping them differently in their mind when writing. If that happens, spend an extra minute to explain that the same areas might have positive and negative factors. It is by understanding how they are related to each other under the same group can we identify improvements.

STARFISH

Think what the team should start, stop or keep doing.

DESCRIPTION

This is a very action-oriented technique that asks the main question of a retrospective "What can be done?" right away. It can be a great tool for mature teams that have good ideas for improvements. It might be more complicated with teams that need a warm-up exercise and a baseline to brainstorm good action items.

This technique can also be used in follow-up retrospective sessions after your team has come up with plenty of ideas that could not be all done in one sprint. It is a great opportunity to revisit all the action items from the previous retrospectives together with the team and come up with new ones.

Duration: **Facilitation difficulty:**   **Team maturity:**

●○○○○   ●○○   ●●●○

WHITEBOARD SETUP

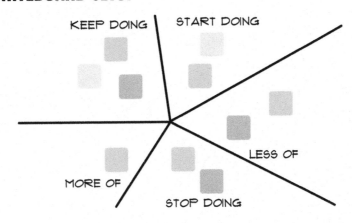

INSTRUCTIONS

1. **Introduce the technique** by explaining what each side of the graph means.

> "In today's session, we will focus on actions that we can undertake to improve our ways of working. As we have worked together for some time and developed a good understanding of the team processes, we can brainstorm on what we can do as a team."

2. **Ask the team to reflect on their past sprint** and write down action items that fit categories of the graph on sticky notes.

> "Look back at the past sprint and think about anything that you wish we would start or stop doing or something that was particularly useful and we should keep doing. On the whiteboard, we have five categories. Here is what they mean:
>
> Keep Doing - something we do well and we recognize the value of it.
>
> Less Of - something we already do; we see some value, but effort spent does not worth it as much; we would rather reduce the effort a little.
>
> More Of - something we already do; and we believe it will bring more value if done even more.
>
> Stop Doing - something that is not bringing value, or even worse, it is getting in the way.
>
> Start Doing - a new idea, or something we have seen working before that we would like to bring to the table.
>
> Keeping these categories in mind when thinking of ideas. Please write one idea per sticky note."

3. **Ask the team members to put their sticky notes on the graph** in the corresponding category.

> *"When you have completed writing your notes, please put them up in the corresponding categories on the board. We will go through all of the notes to see if there are any patterns."*

4. **Go around the graph looking at each category** and discussing the action items suggested. Ask the team what items do they think would bring the most value. If the items suggested are too broad or vague, break them down into more specific action items. At this point, you might want to do a dot voting exercise. Since the technique is focusing on creating action items by default it might be necessary to choose only a subset of the items on the graph.

> *"I will be reading the notes from each category. As we were primarily focusing on action items, we already have a lot of them to discuss. We should think about what items will bring the most value immediately if we decide to implement them next sprint. We should be able to choose a set of actions that make the most sense. If we see an item that is not specific enough, but we think is still very important, we should break it down."*

5. **Ask the team to agree on what action items are the most important** and phrased them in a clear way, ask for volunteers to drive these activities.

6. **Close the session** by thanking the team for sharing their precise ideas about what can be done to improve.

> *"In today's session, we were able to focus on actual action items from the start. If we decided to not take some of the ideas in the next sprint, let's keep them in mind for the future and revisit when it makes sense."*

MODIFICATIONS

Short Version

To make this technique more focused, you can keep only three categories: Start doing, Keep doing and Stop doing.

FACILITATOR NOTES

Sometimes it is difficult to see the difference between "Less of" and "More of". Pay attention to what notes the team comes up with for these categories. When you review the items, try to identify the underlying problem as it will give you better insight into what should be done to improve the situation.

SAILBOAT

Look at the positive and negative factors impacting the team internally versus externally.

DESCRIPTION

This technique focuses on identifying what impacts the team internally versus externally. It helps divide what can be influenced immediately with the team effort and what is out of our control to align expectations on what challenges can be solved faster.

It is a more lightweight version of the Circle of Control technique that is described later in the book. It is a simple exercise to help the team understand that there are some challenges that will either take longer to resolve or cannot be resolved at the time because they come from external sources.

Duration:	Facilitation difficulty:	Team maturity:
●●○○○	●○○	●○○○

WHITEBOARD SETUP

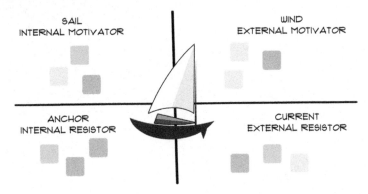

SAIL
INTERNAL MOTIVATOR

WIND
EXTERNAL MOTIVATOR

ANCHOR
INTERNAL RESISTOR

CURRENT
EXTERNAL RESISTOR

INSTRUCTIONS

1. **Introduce the technique** to the group by pointing out the sailboat metaphor.

> *"Let's consider a boat as a metaphor to our past sprint. Our boat was moving forward thanks to different motivators, things that helped, such as a sail that is controlled by the sailors, hence is an internal motivator, but also thanks to the favourable wind which is external to our team. We were facing challenges, such as the anchor that we might have dropped at a wrong time, representing an internal resistor, but also due to adverse current, representing external resistor."*

2. **Ask the team to think about what helped them and what hindered them** during the previous sprint. Different colour sticky notes can be used here. Each idea should be written on a separate note. At this point, the team should not be focusing on whether motivators or resistors are internal or external.

> *"Let's look at the previous sprint as our boat. Think about what helped us on the way and what hindered us. Do not focus on finding internal or external factors, for now, just anything that comes to mind, anything or anyone that you think impacted the progress of our sprint."*

3. **Ask each team member to put the notes up on the graph** - this time they should think about whether each item is external or internal. Group items if necessary.

"Now that you have collected ideas related to the previous sprint, we need to identify where each note sits on the graph: does it come from internal or external factors. Think of internal factors as anything that our team has control over; and external factors - anything that we cannot influence ourselves and that come from other teams or people, within or outside of our organization. Feel free to come up to the whiteboard and put up your notes."

4. **Take note of where you see the most items** and discuss this with the team: why do we see the most notes in this part?

"All of the notes are up on the graph. What patterns do you see? Why do we have a lot of notes in one corner and much less in the other? Usually, it would mean that one factor was much more important in the work we did the last sprint. What was that factor for us?"

5. **Go around the graph starting with internal motivators** and discuss with the team what actions they would like to focus on based on what is written.
   - [For motivators] What helped us succeed? Is there anything we would like to keep doing next sprint to secure this success?
   - [For resistors] What can be done to avoid this next time? What can we do to prepare for this?

"If time permits, we should go over each corner of the graph and discuss the notes you wrote. Let's first focus on internal factors as we have much more control over them and, hence, should be able to find easy solutions that we can implement right away. We should start on a positive note, so let's look at motivators first, then go over resistors. Then we'll move over to the external factors and will discuss whether we can influence external factors or we should plan for the risks they create."

6. Once you have collected enough valuable action items, ask for volunteers to drive these activities during the next sprint.

7. **Close of the session** by looking at how certain things might be external to our work, while we cannot change it, we can prepare and be able to overcome the challenges.

> *"Analyzing whether different factors affecting our work are internal or external helps us understand how to react and prepare for them. If we cannot directly control some external factors, we can plan for them, as we did today. At the same time, some internal factors can be easily overcome by identifying them. By analyzing where various factors affecting our work came from we were able to prepare for the next sprint, and this will help us make it a success."*

MODIFICATIONS

You can use a variety of metaphors for this technique to keep it more engaging, for example, a race car is another metaphor that is used for this retrospective.

FACILITATOR NOTES

The team might look at certain items from an interesting perspective: something that the team has direct control over is marked as an external factor. Discuss these inconsistencies with the team - you might uncover some unexpected concerns.

HOT-AIR BALLOON

Mitigate risks by looking back at the previous sprint and ahead in the future sprint.

DESCRIPTION

This technique focuses on retrospecting as well as looking into the future sprint. It uses the imagery of a hot air balloon and the weather as a metaphor to help the team to identify things that have helped or hindered them in the past and may help or hinder them in the future.

This technique can help uncover risks that can potentially hinder the team's progress based on what they have observed previously.

It can be a good way to help the team plan ahead, not only focus on what has already happened, as it specifically asks the team members to project their work to the next sprint or release.

Duration: **Facilitation difficulty:**   **Team maturity:**

●●○○○   ●○○   ●○○○

WHITEBOARD SETUP

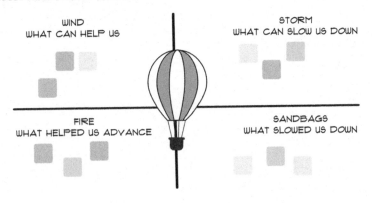

WIND
WHAT CAN HELP US

STORM
WHAT CAN SLOW US DOWN

FIRE
WHAT HELPED US ADVANCE

SANDBAGS
WHAT SLOWED US DOWN

INSTRUCTIONS

1. **Introduce the technique** to the group by explaining the hot-air balloon metaphor.

> *"As we review our previous sprint it would be a good idea to look ahead and plan for the upcoming sprint at the same time. We should be able to base our assumptions for the future sprint after analyzing at what happened during the past sprint."*

2. **Start with the retrospective part by asking the team to look back at the past sprint** and note items that either helped them go higher or propel them forward or pulled them down.

> *"Firstly, we should focus on the past sprint and think about what happened and how it affected our work. What has helped us move towards our goals? What has hindered our progress? Think about any meaningful events that somehow made us go faster or slower."*

3. **Ask the team to place their notes at the bottom part of the hot-air balloon** in the corresponding group (FIRE or SANDBAGS) and have a quick review of what was written down. Group items if necessary. This will align everyone's ideas and will give the team some food for thought for the next part of the session.

> *"To align our ideas we should have a quick overview of everything that you wrote. I invite you to come up to the whiteboard one by one and read your notes out loud. Elaborate on your idea briefly to make sure everyone understands the main idea.*
>
> *If you feel that someone has already brought the same idea up, group the notes together."*

4. **Continue with the futurespective part** by asking the team to consider the information they've collected about past sprint and look to the next sprint. Ask them to think about the following questions:

- What potential risks (storms) can we see ahead that may cause challenges along the way?
- What can help us avoid the risks and overcome possible challenges?

"As we are now all aligned on the past sprint events that have affected our work, we should look into the next sprint so that we can plan for it better. Looking at what happened the last sprint, think about what risks or positive factors might impact our work going forward. Once again, think about things that might help us, but also that might hinder us."

5. **Ask the team to place their notes at the top part of the hot-air balloon** in the corresponding group (WIND or STORM) and have a quick review of what was written down. Group items if necessary.

"Same as in the first part of the session, come up to the whiteboard and place your notes in the corresponding corner. Give a brief description to the team, and group the notes if possible."

6. **Have a group discussion around past events and future risks** and encourage the team to come up with action items to prepare them for the future sprint, especially in order to mitigate identified risks.

> *"We have a full picture now: we have reviewed what has happened in the past sprint and how it might affect our future sprint. Let's discuss what we can see on the graph in more detail. Focus on the patterns you see on the graph, or items that relate to each other. How do past events impact future events and what can we do about it? How can we prepare for the upcoming sprint better looking at the notes you have written? Come up with action items and experiments we can try."*

7. **Close of the session** by pointing out that as we learn new things from the past we should be able to use it to mitigate potential issues in the future which we were able to do using hot-air balloon retrospective technique.

> *"Understanding past events can help us also prepare for potential risks and get the most out of positive factors coming up. In today's session, we were able to analyze the last sprint which in turn allowed us to prepare for the next one. It should help us be more successful next time."*

FACILITATOR NOTES

Another way of conducting the second part of this retrospective is to have an open discussion with the team, especially if you have limited time. Once you've discussed what helped the team and what pulled them down by asking them to write ideas on sticky notes, go directly to the risks. By that time you already should have some action items and areas for improvement. Here ask the team what risks or concerns they envision in getting those things done (thunder, stormy cloud). Write down ideas as they speak. At the same time ask them what can be done to avoid those risks and write down action items for that (sun).

TEAM INDEX

Measure how the team is doing in a variety of areas.

DESCRIPTION

This technique is fully customizable to fit the situations and topics for your team and can be used as a great follow-up tool to see how the team is improving and can be used to access team maturity. By using this technique the team will be able to evaluate a variety of areas that impact their work and plan for ways to solve issues and endure successes. You can track the progress of each area by using this technique once every quarter, for example, which will give an opportunity to set specific improvement goals for the team.

Duration:	Facilitation difficulty:	Team maturity:
●●●○○	●○○	●●●○

Concept:

Squad Health Check model by Henrik Kniberg: (https://labs.spotify.com/2014/09/16/squad-health-check-model/).

WHITEBOARD SETUP

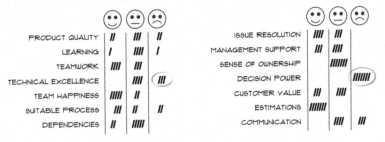

	😊	😐	😞			😊	😐	😞
PRODUCT QUALITY	//	///	//		ISSUE RESOLUTION	////	///	
LEARNING	/	////	/		MANAGEMENT SUPPORT	///	////	
TEAMWORK	////	///			SENSE OF OWNERSHIP	//////		
TECHNICAL EXCELLENCE		////	(///)		DECISION POWER			(//////)
TEAM HAPPINESS	/////	//			CUSTOMER VALUE	///	////	
SUITABLE PROCESS	///	//	//		ESTIMATIONS	///////		
DEPENDENCIES	//	/////			COMMUNICATION	////	///	

Topics and descriptions

Topic	Green	Red
Knowledge Availability	Experts are always available to answer our questions. We never have to wait for the necessary information.	We don't really know who to ask, and even if we know they are usually unavailable and we have to wait to get answers.
Product Clarity	We know exactly what the long-term roadmap looks like. We're excited about our future product.	It's unclear what the product is going towards. We don't have visibility on what we're going to work on next.
Issue Resolution	When issues come up, we quickly resolve them thanks to team agreements established earlier.	We don't know how to deal with issues effectively. Each team member tends to resolve things on their own and avoids talking about them.
Ownership	We are dedicated to delivering our work and feel responsible for getting things done right.	We just follow processes. Someone else will make sure we do things right.
Learning	We're learning interesting new technologies and new ways of doing things with every feature we develop.	We rarely have time to learn anything new. Nothing really to tell developer friends about anyway.
Decisions	We are fully in control of the feature work. We decide how to build new features by following general guidelines.	Most of the time we are told what approach to take exactly in building new features. There's no room for creativity.

Dependencies	We get stuff done really quickly, we are rarely delayed by others external to the team.	We keep getting stuck or interrupted and we have a hard time to complete story work quickly.
Suitable Process	Processes in place help us get our work done faster and easier. This way of working is the most effective.	Processes get in our way and make us lose precious time.
Customer Value	We know what positive impact our products have on our customers as we get their feedback every time.	It's not clear whether what we deliver is what our customer really want as we have no way to get feedback from them.
Team Happiness	We love coming to work, people are fun and inspiring. You can often hear laughter in our workspace.	Work is work. Usually, our days are pretty dull, almost nobody ever laughs.
Estimations	Our estimations are perfect. We know exactly how much effort each story will take us, we know how to incorporate risks and uncertainties in estimates as well.	Our estimations are wonky, we tend to over or underestimate most of the stories, especially in terms of risks and uncertainties.
Teamwork	We always effectively share work and collaborate. We know how to work with each other for the best results. We are a team.	We are just a collection of individuals, we work in silos. We don't know how to share work or collaborate effectively.
Technical Excellence	We're proud of the quality of our team code. It is clean, easy to read and has great test coverage. We even refactor!	Our code can definitely use a lot more test coverage and reviews. Technical debt is raging out of control.

Cross-team Communication	We actively engage other teams and management into discussions, even if there's an issue.	Each team works in a silo. We do not communicate proactively with other teams. They do their stuff, we do ours.

INSTRUCTIONS

1. **Introduce the technique** as a way to measure current team state and plan improvements. It is also a way to check if the changes we make in our ways of working help us in certain areas or not by measuring the same area again several months later.

> *"In today's session, we will be able to access our current state and understand what areas we should focus on going forward. It is a great way to evaluate a number of different processes and practices. As time goes on, we will be able to come back to this evaluation and review what we have achieved.*
>
> *I also envision some interesting revelations coming up as some of you might have different views on the same topics".*

2. **Distribute voting cards** and explain that you will be reading out statements for each area of improvement and each team member will need to vote using the cards. The statements you will be reading are for the two extremes: green state and red state.

> *"Each person will have an opportunity to vote. We can do anonymous voting if you would like where I only calculate the number of votes, but you don't have to show the votes to the team. Otherwise, everybody can show their votes at the same time to each other, as we do during estimations with planning poker.*

> *About the voting itself: I will be reading out statements for each topic. One statement will represent the ideal state. If you believe we are in the ideal state or are close to it, then vote with your green card. The second statement will represent the worst case scenario. If you feel we are close to that state, then vote with your red card. If you are unsure or feel that the team is somewhere in the middle, then vote with a yellow card."*

3. **Write down the name of the first area you want to measure** in the table you prepared. Read the description of green state and red state to the team. Remember to say "Green" or "Red" before the statements to help the team understand what state each statement refers to.

> *"Let's start with knowledge availability. Green: experts are always available to answer our questions. We never have to wait for the necessary information. Or red: we don't really know who to ask, and even if we know they are usually unavailable and we have to wait to get answers."*

4. **Ask the team to show their votes with the cards.** Calculate how many votes of each colour you have and note it in the table in front of the area name. Either during the session or afterwards, you can calculate the weighted average score. For example, count red a 1, yellow as 2 and green as 3. With a team of 6 people, if you have 2 votes for each color, you will calculate: $(1*2 + 2*2 + 3*2)/6 = 2$ weighted average. With a weighted average, it will be much easy to see trends in each category when you evaluate it next time. I encourage you to spend some extra time on that. You can even create graphs that you can display in the team area as an encouragement for improvement.

> *"Hold the card with your vote up: green, yellow or red. I'll calculate the total number of votes. Don't be surprised if your vote is drastically different from other team members - we will be able to discuss it later on. Each of us has a different vision on the situation or has a specific reason to give it a certain vote."*

5. **Continue in the same way for the rest of the areas** you would like to evaluate.

"We will not be discussing the votes just yet - we will finish voting on all areas and then we'll identify what areas to talk about depending on the total score."

6. **Look on the positive side** and identify the areas with the most positive votes - congratulate the team on achieving positive results in the areas. You will not spend a lot of time looking into these areas, therefore, it is important to briefly highlight them.

"Let's acknowledge the good work we did on areas with the most positive votes. Would anyone like to talk about some of the positive things that we have accomplished? For example, here we have the most green votes. What made it such a success? Is there anything that surprised you during voting? For example, if someone put a completely different vote from yours. Let's discuss it briefly."

7. **Identify what areas have the most negative votes** and outline them as the most important to focus on. Depending on the number of items to discuss and the time you have left, define whether you are going to cover all of them or conduct dot voting.

"Now that we have a clear picture on all the areas it is easy to spot the ones that require our attention. Let's look at the areas that got the most red votes and think about the ways to improve. Since we know that these areas are not doing great, we are sure to spend our time there where it would make the most positive impact. Our goal is to level out all areas across the table."

8. **Facilitate the discussion around each area**, think about the underlying reasons for current state and potential improvements that the team can make.

> *"Starting off with this area, let me read to you the ideal state and the worst case scenario to give a reminder of why we put these votes here (read the explanations once again for the chosen area).*
>
> *Why do you think it is in a bad shape? What are the primary reasons? Think about both internal and external reasons that are affecting this. Is the situation under our control or someone outside of our team is influencing it?"*

9. **As you discuss each area and come up with some action items**, ask the team what do they want to work on first and what can be actually accomplished in the upcoming sprint. Ask for volunteers to drive various action items you've identified.

10. **Close the retrospective** with another overall look at the current state of areas you measured. Tell the team that together you have committed to improving on certain areas and you will do another evaluation in a couple of months to see your progress.

> *"In today's session, we were able to evaluate ourselves in a number of different important areas. It is a great start to keep us on track of continuous improvement. Now we know where to focus our efforts going forward. In addition, we will be able to come back to this evaluation in a couple of months and look at our progress. Let's keep the areas of improvement in mind when we meet again in our next retrospective."*

MODIFICATIONS

One to five.

As I've seen with some teams, the 3-scale range might seem not enough. If your team feels they are somewhat ok with everything, you might have mostly yellows in your votes. In this case switch the technique to using 5-scale vote: 1 would represent red and 5 would represent green (or vice versa). You will need a separate set of voting cards for that.

FACILITATOR NOTES

Depending on current team dynamics, you might want to conduct the evaluation anonymously where every person puts their card face down and only you as facilitator can see the notes team members give. The team will only see a consolidated result and will not know who voted for what.

Some team members tend to vote yellow even if in truth they feel it should be red. Often it is because the statements provided for the state in red are quite negative. You might want to change the description to something more neutral if this happens or use "One to five" modification.

It is helpful to calculate the average result for each area as it is easier to compare them in the future.

PEOPLE & PROCESS

Identify areas of improvement related to people, relationships, process and tools.

DESCRIPTION

This technique is based on the standard approach described in the Scrum Guide and focuses on defining improvements in regards to people, relationships, processes and tools.

This is an easy way to start discussions around the most common areas and give instant ideas to your team of what to look at when thinking about potential improvements.

This technique can be used with a team of any level of maturity, and it is especially effective with the teams which had never done a retrospective before.

Duration: **Facilitation difficulty:**   **Team maturity:**

●●●○○   ●○○   ●○○○

WHITEBOARD SETUP

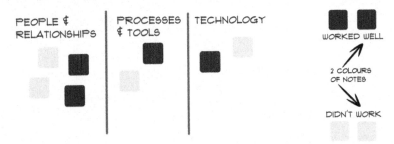

INSTRUCTIONS

1. **Introduce the technique** by referring to the Scrum Guide:

> *"The Sprint retrospective is an opportunity for the Scrum Team to inspect itself and create a plan for improvements to be enacted during the next Sprint. One of the purposes of the retrospective is to inspect how the last Sprint went with regards to people, relationships, process, and tools. These are the categories we will be focusing on today. It is a quite basic approach, and it helps to cover all the most important areas from a high level."*

2. **Distribute two colours of sticky notes and ask the team to brainstorm** on what went well (one colour) and what didn't go well (another colour) the last sprint in relation to each of the categories.

> *"Think about what happened during the last sprint, what work we did and what practices we followed. Write things that went well on blue notes, and what didn't go so well on red notes. Write one idea per note. Even small things can be valuable to our discussion. Don't focus on the categories just yet and don't discard any ideas. Write down whatever comes to mind when thinking about the past sprint."*

3. **Ask the team to put up the notes in the table** according to the category. Read the notes out loud and group them if necessary.

> *"Feel free to go to the board and put your notes up in one of the categories: people and relationships, processes and tools, or technology.*

> *People and relationships category is related to how we interact within the team, with other teams or management. This category represents communication. Processes and tools category is related to the way we work, what practices we follow, how we deal with incidents or support request, how we plan, and other processes. Technology category is related to the technical side of our work, the quality of our code, our design and architecture, all things technical."*

4. **Highlight the category that has the most positive notes**, and congratulate the team on achieving great results in this area.

> *"I can see that this category has the most positive notes. It means that we are doing a lot of good things here and we should continue that. It is a great achievement, let's recognize it."*

5. **Highlight the category that has the most notes identified as 'needs improvement'.** Start the discussion around what went wrong and what can be done to change that in the future. Your goal is to help the team come up with action items to try.

> *"This particular category needs the most attention. A lot of you have marked that things didn't go well in relation to this area of work. Let's review what kind of challenges we have faced during the last sprint. Do you see any patterns? Are any challenges related to each other or have the same underlying reason?*
>
> *What can we do to improve? If we have identified the reason, how can we influence it to make the situation better next time?"*

6. **Move on to the next category** and repeat until you cover all of them.

> *"Let's look at the other category and answer the same question as we did in the previous step. How can we improve in this area? Is there anything specific that can be done by the team?"*

7. **Choose the activities to focus on the next sprint** and ask for volunteers to drive them. It would be best if you have an action item for each category.

8. **Close the session** by bringing attention to the importance of the different aspects of team's work: as they continuously improve in one area they should always keep improving in another to align the level of team maturity across all areas.

> *"In today's session, we were able to cover the most basic and the most important areas of our work aligned with how the Scrum Guide recommends looking at it. In helped us uncover where we are at now and focus our improvement efforts on the areas that face the most challenges. This will allow us to align our ways of working in all areas and will help us become more agile."*

MODIFICATIONS

Other categories

The technique can give different results if you slightly change the categories to attract attention to different parts of the process. For example, try the following categories instead: communication, practices, product.

FACILITATOR NOTES

If your team feels that some topics they would like to discuss do not fit in any category, you may want to adjust your table and add a new category that works best.

Another way of doing it is to start the session by defining the categories together with the team by giving them examples of different categories that can be used in this exercise.

MEDIUM FACILITATION TECHNIQUES

As you start getting more familiar with your team and with retrospective facilitation, you should give a try to new techniques from this section of the book.

Most of the techniques here will allow you to bring fresh discussions into your retrospectives which will, in turn, need stronger facilitation. It can be related to discussions and debates going in the wrong direction or to your team not understanding how to come to useful conclusions and action items.

Some of the techniques will need more detailed explanations and examples. Most of them will also require extra-preparation to help you answer questions during the session.

EXPECTATIONS

Compare team expectations of the past sprint and the actual outcomes.

DESCRIPTION

This technique helps the team align their expectations of the previous sprint and understand whether those expectations were met. The second part of this technique focuses on planning for next sprint expectations and enabling the team to meet them. It can be used with teams of any level of Agile maturity. It is also possible to make this session very short if you are pressed for time.

Setting expectations is an important part of agile and this technique might help the team uncover that they are not aligned on what they can accomplish as a team or on the quality of their work or other important aspects. This can also help the team understand whether they expect too much or too little of each other. Be careful with this technique if your team has trust issues as it might create some tension between the teammates - facilitate the discussion with care.

Duration:	Facilitation difficulty:	Team maturity:
●○○○○	●●○	●○○○

WHITEBOARD SETUP

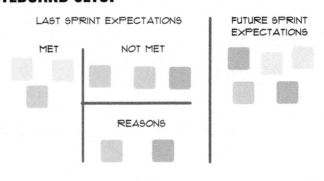

69

INSTRUCTIONS

1. **Start the retrospective** by presenting the need to set the right expectations in order to properly plan ahead.

> *"As we enter each sprint we have certain expectations about how our work is going to progress and what result we are trying to achieve. Sometimes it is expressed in our sprint goal. Sometimes it goes beyond the work we do and relates to personal relationships, communication and processes that we follow. Whatever our expectations are, we often do not realize that each one of us might have a different set of expectations and it is important to recognize all of them as this will help us understand whether our expectations were met from different perspectives."*

2. **Ask the team to think about what they expected of this sprint** whether it relates to specific outcomes or ways of work. Each team member can write their ideas on sticky notes, one idea per note. Allow 5 minutes for this activity.

> *"Think about what you expected from the last sprint. It can be a particular piece of functionality finished, or a communication happening, or maybe you hoped to attend a conference. Maybe you had some expectations in regards to your teammates. Include anything you were thinking of at the beginning of the sprint when it started."*

3. **Ask the team to come up to the board and put up their notes** either under "Met" column or "Not met" columns depending on how they feel about these expectations. They can put their notes in between the two columns if they are not sure.

> *"Now that you have collected your ideas about what you have expected from the previous sprint, put notes in a corresponding column depending on whether your expectation was met or not. It will allow us to see the patterns around how are sprint really went aside from the work that we have done.*

4. **Quickly go through the expectations that were met** to recognize the team's success. At the same time check if everyone on the team agrees with this - sometimes team members have a different perspective on the same items. If something is not aligned, have a quick discussion with the team regarding it.

> *"Let's review the expectations in the Met column. If you see something that you do not agree with, we should discuss as a team: there might be some nuances to each expectation and we will be able to discover it during the discussion.*
>
> *But most importantly, let's recognize our success in meeting these expectations."*

5. **Look at the other column with expectations that were not met**, read them out loud and group together if possible. Facilitate a discussion with the team to identify the reasons these expectations were not met.

> *"Now that we have looked at the positive things that happened the last sprint, we should review what didn't go so well: the expectations that were not met. I will read them out loud. The first thing we should do is group them if the expectations are related to each other or are related to the same area.*
>
> *As we review each expectation, think about these questions: Was this expectation reasonable? Did it make sense to plan for it the last sprint? Why did we have this expectation in the first place?"*

6. **As you discuss previous points, take notes** to help make team decisions later on. Your list should gradually expand to two more columns: reasons for not meeting expectations and expectations for next sprint.

> *"With groups of expectations identified, we need to understand how to plan for the future sprint knowing what we know now. Let's discuss each group of expectations and answer these questions: What prevented us from fulfilling this expectation? Were there external factors involved? I will write the answers in the "Reasons" column.*
>
> *If this is something that we would still expect to happen next sprint, what would that look like exactly? Let's write it down in the "Future expectations" column."*

7. **Put some more focus on future expectations.** Ask "Is there anything else that we would expect to happen next sprint?" The last column might not be based solely on past expectations, the team might have new things to add after the discussion.

> *"With some expectations identified from the last sprint, is there anything else that we would expect from the future sprint? Think about other things that we would like to see happen next sprint. As long as we have our expectations set and agreed upon, it will be much easier to plan for them."*

8. **Ask the team to review the notes in two new columns.** It is time to move towards planning out next sprint and thinking about what can be done to meet new expectations and prevent them from not being met. Your previous discussion is a perfect guide for this as it gives you a full picture of what happened in the past sprint.

> *"Let's review our notes so far. Now that we know what exactly what happened in the last sprint and what were the reasons for it, we can start planning for meeting our expectations for the next sprint. Looking at what we expect to happen, how can we make sure that we meet this expectation? What should we do as a team? Is there any preparation that is required from our side?"*

9. **As your team thinks of action items and experiments to try in the next sprint**, ask for volunteers to drive those actions. Keep the list short and focused on the more important things, use voting if necessary.

10. **Close the session** by reminding the team that as we aligned our expectations it will be easier to meet them, especially, with the plan at hand.

> *"In today's session, we had an opportunity to inspect our expectations much closer than we usually do. It was a great opportunity for alignment. With our expectations set for the next sprint, we will be able to quickly see whether we are on the right track for meeting them. This is how we will be able to improve and see our progress in doing so.."*

MODIFICATIONS

I expect from YOU...

You can highlight the expectations we have for different groups of people in the organization if you want to focus your discussion on communication.

In this case, talk about how we sometimes have specific expectations of others, but might not communicate it clearly. Which is why it is important to understand where we need to put more communication efforts to meet our expectations.

Ask a question "What did you expect from ... ?" and write down different groups of people to think about: our organization, our Scrum team, our

Product Owner, our Scrum Master, other teams, management. You can add specific groups, if it makes sense, for example, customer support team.

FACILITATOR NOTES

If the discussion about reasons for expectations not being met starts to revolve around things that the team has no control or influence on, shift the focus onto the expectations for the future sprint. This should bring the team back to the positive and hopeful thinking that will be more productive in defining the action items.

EMOTIONS & TRIGGERS

Identify the impact Sprint Events have on your team happiness.

DESCRIPTION

This technique focuses on the ways team members felt and what triggered those emotions during the sprint. By using this technique you can help the team understand how well sprint events went from a personal point of view of each team member and identify why they felt what they felt. It switches the focus from problems first to the team happiness and will allow the team to understand what really triggers their behaviours during the sprint.

It can be seen as too touchy-feely by some team members, so you will need to set some expectation around it before the start.

Duration: **Facilitation difficulty:**   **Team maturity:**

●●●●○   ●●○   ●●●●○

WHITEBOARD SETUP

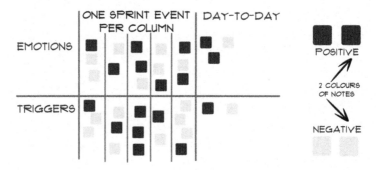

Concept:

Chris Beaudoin, Scrum Master. The idea came from a study conducted by the National Health Service (NHS) in the UK.

INSTRUCTIONS

1. **Describe the purpose of this technique** and explain the graph. Ask the team if they would like to add a column for something specific (for example, if you have regular code review sessions or something similar).

> *"This technique is based on a study conducted to better understand and design processes for hospital patients by looking at all the interactions they have with the solution developed. Today's retrospective will be based on this idea as we'll be reviewing our usual interactions within the team during a regular sprint. In the table on the whiteboard, you can see all the usual Sprint interactions we have as a team. What we will be focusing on is how you felt during those interactions to later identify what triggered these emotions.*
>
> *I have added each sprint event separately as well as a column for our day-to-day work.*
>
> *First of, apart from these typical interactions we have during the sprint, do we want to add any other types of interactions?"*

2. **Allow the team some time to write down emotions for each interaction last sprint.** Ask them to write one word per sticky note choosing the colour depending on whether the emotions are positive or negative. They can have as many sticky notes per interaction as needed.

> *"To start, let's look at the interactions we had during the past sprint and think about how we felt in relation to each one of them. Did you feel mostly negative emotions or did you feel good after attending the event? Since it sometimes might be difficult to find the right word to describe emotions, I have prepared a list of positive and negative emotion words you can use.*
>
> *To have a better visualization, we will use green colour sticky notes for positive emotions and triggers, and red colour sticky notes for negative ones. Think of any emotions that you remember, you might have experienced several different emotions during the same sprint event, both positive and negative - it is totally ok, list all of them."*

3. **Ask the team to put up their sticky notes up on the whiteboard** under corresponding interactions. Make a note of which Sprint interactions have the most negative and which ones have most positive notes. Let everyone review the state of the whiteboard.

> *"When you finished writing notes, please put them up on the board in the corresponding column. We will be able to see patterns between different events: some events will be mostly positive, some other events will have more negative emotions associated with them. This is how we'll know the general state of each interaction.*
>
> *Let's review what we see. Is there anything that surprises you? Is there anything that makes sense because of something specific that happened?"*

4. **Ask the team to think about what triggered the different emotions** they had during different interactions. Each emotion can have several triggers and each trigger can have several emotions related to it, it will not be a 1:1 match. Allow a bit more time for this activity.

"Now that we understand how we felt during each sprint event, we should figure out what triggered those emotions. We will use the coloured notes the same way: green for positive, red for negative. Think about what exactly made you feel the way you felt during the event. You might have several triggers for a single emotion or one trigger for several emotions you've identified before.

If you are not what exactly was the trigger, think about what happened right before, maybe even before the sprint event started."

5. **Ask the team to put up their trigger sticky notes up on the whiteboard.** As they add notes, group them together, if it makes sense.

"As you finish writing what triggered your emotions, please come up to the board and put your notes in the corresponding column. We will see even more interesting patterns as some events might have fewer triggers than emotions in the end. One single thing can spiral out of control very quickly, and we will be able to identify it easily.

If you see the notes that are related, group them together right away. I will also go through the notes quickly to group them where possible."

6. **First look at the areas that are doing well,** where you see the most positive emotions and triggers. Discuss with the team what they should keep doing to keep the positive vibe in this interaction. The team might decide to turn these into action items.

"Firstly, let's look at the positive triggers. What are the positive emotional triggers that you see the most of? There can be some patterns in the way positive triggers affect every sprint event or we can see something very specific to a particular interaction. Is it something that happens thanks to the team's actions? What should we continue doing to keep the positive things happen in our sprint events?

What interaction seems to be the most positive? Why do you think that is?"

7. **Next look at areas that can be improved**, where you see the most negative emotions and triggers. Discuss what is causing the most challenges with this interaction and encourage the team to identify solutions: what can we do to improve this event?

"Now let's look at the areas that need improvement. What sprint event suffers the most? We should discuss why this is happening and what can we do to improve it. What are the underlying reasons for many negative emotions and triggers? What are the first steps in making this interaction more enjoyable going forward? How can we as a team create a positive impact?"

8. **Ask the team to choose the most important action items** to focus on the next sprint. Let the team members volunteer to drive the chosen action items.

9. **Close the session** by highlighting the fact that different emotions can be triggered by the same thing and one thing can trigger a variety of emotions. Knowing what caused us to feel a certain way can help us be more aware of ourselves and find new ways to improve.

> *"In today's session, we were able to identify how we felt in relation to different team interactions that happen during the sprint and find underlying causes or triggers. It was a great exercise to understand what really drives the way we work and interact with each other from a point of view that we often overlook. Going forward it will be easier to recognize how we can positively impact how satisfied we are with the way our sprint goes."*

MODIFICATIONS

Happiness index

If your team is struggling to find the right words for emotions, replace emotions with a happiness index with three possibilities: happy, average, and sad. Just adding simple smiley faces can go a long way to help your team open up about how they feel.

Ways of interaction

You can use this technique for categories other than sprint events, especially, when you would like to focus team's attention on certain issues. In this case, change the columns to the categories you need, such as estimation, collaboration, engagement, or other areas that you feel would be useful to cover.

FACILITATOR NOTES

With a new team, this technique can help you uncover some long lasting inefficiencies in your sprint events and allow you to improve your Agile processes. Though you need to be aware of a level of trust required to run this technique successfully. If you feel that there are some trust issues within your team, it would be best to address them first, as this technique might easily bring judgemental attitudes into the room.

It is extremely useful to have some emotion words ready for your team. Many teams are struggling to identified relevant emotion words during the first part of the exercise and leave only simplified versions of them (like, happy or sad). Allow your team to be more specific by preparing a list of words that they can draw inspiration from.

RESOLUTIONS

Make a plan on how to improve in areas identified by the team.

DESCRIPTION

This technique will help the team to focus on main areas of improvement and draft an action plan. It will also help each team member think about how they can contribute to team improvements based on their general team dynamics and team health by identifying main pain points first.

It is a great start for a new team to understand where they are in terms of processes, communication and other important elements of teamwork. This can also be a great exercise to do at the beginning of a year, quarter or a release window. It would also help to go back to the outputs of this retrospective as a guide for future improvements.

Duration:	Facilitation difficulty:	Team maturity:
●●●●●	●●○	●○○○

WHITEBOARD SETUP

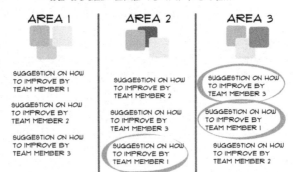

INSTRUCTIONS

1. **Introduce the technique** to the team to get them excited about making team resolutions for the future.

> "People make New Year resolutions in order to become better, feel better and improve their lives in general. Today we'll be making resolutions on how to improve our team and will work together towards accomplishing them. As a team we have all the necessary information about where we can improve, that is why all the content created in today's session will be based on your own observations."

2. **Ask each team member to write what they think** are the main areas of improvement for the team on a sticky note. It should be represented in a single phrase. Each team member should write down no more than one to two ideas. The team should not write specific action items, for now, only general areas where the team could improve.

> "We'll spend some individual time to come up with ideas. Write down one or two areas of improvement you think we should focus on in the upcoming sprints. If you have more ideas, choose maximum two that you think are the most important ones. Do not write action items, meaning, do not start your phrase with a verb, use nouns instead.
>
> If you have a very specific example, like, 'our Planning events are too long' or 'we need to do code reviews', instead write 'Sprint Planning effectiveness' or 'Code quality' as areas of improvement. Good areas of improvement could be: estimation, collaboration with external teams, team morale, etc. Think of areas that are the most impactful on the way the team works."

3. **Collect the notes and read them aloud**. Group the areas of improvement into topics if possible or if necessary and name those topics in a couple of words.

At the end, you should have no more than five areas of improvement.

> *"I will read all listed areas of improvement and we should group them along the way. Our goal is to have no more than five areas of improvement identified, otherwise, we will spread our efforts too thin and will not be able to get bigger enough impact to improve our ways of work.*
>
> *Anything that does not align with an existing group and becomes a standalone, most likely will be put aside for the rest of the discussion, unless you think it is actually more important than something else.*
>
> *As we group all notes together where possible, let's name each group with an appropriate area of improvement. A good name will perfectly finish a sentence 'We would like to improve ...' or 'We would like to improve how we do ...'"*

4. **Assign each area of improvement to a different team member for the first round**. If you have too many team members, assign more to each area. If there are not enough people to cover all areas, ask them to do the exercise for more areas at once. Ask each team member to write down one single action item they would like to take towards the area of improvement they are assigned to - their first resolution.

> *"Now it is the time for the team to decide what can be done to make positive changes in each area. Each one of you should take a marker and choose an group to start with. Try to spread around the board so that each group has at least one person looking at it.*
>
> *In the next two or three minutes, write down under the group name one action item you think we should do as a team next sprint to make an improvement in this area. Then we'll rotate."*

5. **Ask the team to rotate around the room** and write next resolution on a different area of improvement. You may do a free rotation where the

team is free to walk around and contribute resolutions to whatever area they want. Otherwise, you can organize the rotation by giving everyone 2 minutes on each area, then rotate to the next one, etc. Continue this for around 10 minutes to gather insight.

> *"Let's rotate. Move to the next group to your right and spend the next two minutes adding an action item to work on to improve in the area that you are in front of now. The previous action item can be a good reference for you and might help you come up with a more refined idea for the same action item, in this case, add your comments all the same.*
>
> *Once we finish, we'll rotate again, until everyone had a chance to review each area of improvement and contribute their action item ideas."*

6. **Finish rotation**. If you're using paper ask team members to read the resolutions aloud from each paper. Otherwise, give everyone some time to read flipchart and whiteboard notes.

> *"We are finishing the rotation. Now that everyone had a chance to contribute to each area of improvement, let's review all the notes. If you have any question in regards to certain action items, please ask them right away. We should all understand what each action item means."*

7. **Conduct dot voting for the whole list of resolutions** across all areas of improvement. Highlight the resolutions that got the most votes. It's up to you and the team to decide how many you want to focus on.

> *"Because we have several areas of improvement and each person on the team was able to contribute to the action items, we have collected a good amount of ideas. Unfortunately, we won't be able to accomplish all of them. We need to focus our efforts on what will bring the most value with the least amount of effort to kick-start our improvements. Let's spend a couple of minutes voting on the specific actions we would like to focus on in the next sprint. Each of you will have 5 votes. You can put all of the votes on one action, distribute between different actions. We are voting on actual action items, not areas of improvement."*

8. **Ask the team to think about specific actions** to be taken right away for each resolution chosen, especially if it is very big or vague. What risks and concerns are related to them? How to avoid those risks? Ask for volunteers to the action items.

> *"Based on the votes we have some clear action items that seem to be the most valuable and important to the team. Let's make sure we understand what the next step exactly is and find volunteers to drive the action."*

9. **Close the retrospective** by congratulating the team on making the resolutions to become better and encourage them to stick to their plan to see great results in the end.

> *"Today we had a great opportunity to look at what we can improve as a team of a higher level by identifying areas of improvement rather than specific challenges. This will be a good guide for us to review our progress going forward and also a good input for our future retrospectives. Let's keep in mind all the areas of improvement that we have identified today, still focusing on the action items that we have chosen during the session."*

MODIFICATIONS

Categorization

Instead of identifying the areas of improvements first, ask the team to make resolutions directly based on predefined categories. Team members will write their resolutions for each category. This allows a more broad perspective and might give you different results than looking at it from areas of improvement perspective.

FACILITATOR NOTES

To make sure areas of improvement are not mixed up with actual action items, ask the team to not use verbs and use nouns instead when writing down areas of improvement. Ask them to make it brief, no more than 2-4 words. Otherwise, you might end up with very specific action items that cannot be used in this exercise.

Read up on previous retrospectives to define main areas of improvements in case the team is having a hard time defining them at the beginning of the session.

SUCCESS STORIES

Measure how successful the team is in their planning activities.

DESCRIPTION

Success stories can help the team identify how well they plan their work as well as see whether their planning is actually successful or not. It looks at all the meaningful events through the lens of whether they were planned or unexpected and whether they made positive or negative impact on the team's work.

This technique can help you show patterns between the way team plans and what outcomes they get at the end.

It is best to use this technique with a team that has run together for a while as they need to have some experience with planning their sprints and reviewing them in retrospectives.

It might be difficult to facilitate this technique at first as discussions tend to become long, therefore, leave enough time for this retrospective technique at first.

Duration:	Facilitation difficulty:	Team maturity:
●●●○○	●●○	●●●○

WHITEBOARD SETUP

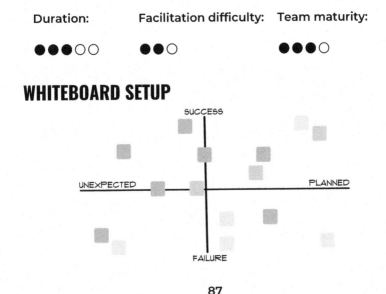

INSTRUCTIONS

1. **Introduce the goal of the retrospective** and explain each quadrant on the chart.

> *"Planning is an important part of our sprints. The better we plan, the more predictable is our work and easier it is to set up expectations with our customers. While we cannot plan everything in advance, as long as we stay consistent our predictability will increase.*
>
> *In today's retrospective we will be able to review how successful we are in our planning activities"*

2. **Give the team some time to individually write what happened** during the last iteration: any events that impacted the team's work, goals that they set up, tasks they ended up doing. Encourage them to think in terms of successes and failures only. You can also use different colours for different outcomes.

> *"Let's spend some time identifying all meaningful activities that happened last sprint. Don't just think of events that happened, such as 'a build failed' - it is an event that happened, but not an activity we planned as a team. In this case, you might think of something like 'fixing our build took us too long' which is an unsuccessful activity we performed. Think of all the activities, whether successful or failed. For now, do not over-analyze them, do not consider if we plan for those activities or not, just think of the outcomes different activities had."*

3. **Ask the team to put up their sticky notes on the board**. This time they should put the notes depending not only on the outcome but also think about how well planned this activity was. In this case, planning means that the team expected to do this activity or it was supposed to happen. If the team completed the previous step correctly, they will not have issues placing the items in the correct categories.

"In the first part, we have defined successful and unsuccessful activities and events. Now looking at the chart, think about how did we prepare for them. We do not plan for failures, but it might just happen that we knew it was going to happen, or an unsuccessful activity happened only because we did not plan well the work that was required to complete a user story, for example. Going back to the build example, we can say that we have planned to be fixing our build - we know it breaks and we planned some time to do it, however, the activity itself was unsuccessful, therefore, it will appear under 'Planned but failed' category. Or for example, we ended up having to do some refactoring that we did not plan for and it for, unfortunately, unsuccessful as it broke something in our codebase. This activity will appear in the 'Unexpected and failed' category.

Please take your notes and put them up on the board according to how well planned or unplanned was the activity, and how successful or unsuccessful it was."

4. **Look at your graph and together with the team group any items** where possible. Ask the team what patterns they see on the graph: are there a lot of unplanned and failed activities or planned and successful ones?

"To facilitate the next part of the discussion, let's group the activities where possible. I'll quickly review the notes, let me know which activities should go together.

Is there anything that surprises you? Do you see any patterns in one side of the graph?"

5. **Go around the board counter-clockwise starting with planned and successful** activities. Facilitate the discussion around the way these activities came to be in this part of the graph. Questions should be encouraging enough for the team to come up with action items for the next sprint. Write their ideas as they discuss.

"Let's start discussing what we have put on the graph in more detail. We will start with the top right corner with planned and successful activities and will go counter-clockwise. Looking at these activities we can assume that we did a good job planning for them since they also turned to be successful. How did we plan for this activity? Why was it a success? Was the fact that we planned for it a reason for success?"

6. **Continue the discussion around unexpected but successful** activities.

"Continuing our discussion, we can go to unexpected but successful activities. How did we achieve success with this activity without planning it? Is it something that can be planned for? How can we prepare ourselves better for unexpected activities to make them successful? How do we ensure our success next time?"

7. **Continue the discussion around unexpected and failed** activities.

"Next we should look at unexpected activities that were not successful. Since these actions led to negative results, we really need to understand, what led to this and how we can avoid this from happening next time. What was the reason we could not plan for it? What could be the outcome, if we planned for it properly?"

8. **Finish the discussion** on planned but failed activities.

> *"To finish our discussion, let's review activities that we planned for but were not able to achieve success with. It is important to learn from failures and plan to remediate them in the future sprint. Looking at the activities in this part of the graph, what did we miss when we planned for them that failed us? How can we plan better next time?"*

9. With a list of action items, **discuss what actions** are the most important and highlight them on the board to pick-up for the next iteration.

10. **Close the session** by reminding the team that planning ahead can help them get more successes out of activities.

> *"In today's retrospective, we were able to review how well we plan our sprints and understand if the way we plan impacts our success. The more consistent we are with planning our sprints, the easier it will be to predict the outcome and we'll be faced with fewer surprises at the end of the sprint."*

MODIFICATIONS

Categorization

Before the team starts writing notes, define categories they should think in. Usual categories to use: people & communication, technology, organization & process, other. Use different colour notes for each category.

FACILITATOR NOTES

Make note of same events that appear under different quadrants - it means the team is not aligned with planning activities and their definition of success. If team members can see the same things differently, it is important to encourage the discussion. Why did one person think it was planned, whereas another one thought of it as something unexpected? This might uncover some communication issues and lead to good action items.

SPRINT TIMELINE

Review the last sprint timeline and analyze how events impacted the team's work.

DESCRIPTION

This technique is a great way to look back, even on longer periods of time and analyze the most important events that happened. When you prepare it correctly, you can use it as a Release retrospective.

As the team looks at the past sprint (or release), they can identify what happened and how it impacted their progress towards their goals and come up with solutions for the future.

This technique will be a great help in case the team struggled with unexpected issues occurring during development.

Duration:	Facilitation difficulty:	Team maturity:
●●●●●	●●○	●●●○

WHITEBOARD SETUP

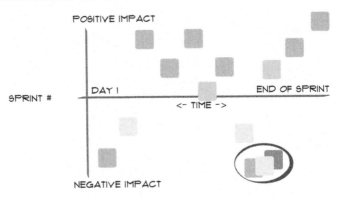

INSTRUCTIONS

1. **Start by introducing the goals of this session** and pointing out the timeline view that the team will be using to analyze the past sprint.

> *"When we are used to running fast, as in, doing our work in sprints, it is sometimes difficult to stop and look back, but it is necessary in order to analyze everything that happened in more details.*
>
> *Let's have a deep dive into our past sprint/two sprints/release/quarter/etc. To help us with this task, we'll create a timeline that shows everything that happened and made an impact on our work, whether positive or negative. We will be able to review the work done from everyone's perspective and use it to plan for improvements in the future sprints."*

2. **Ask the team to think about various memorable events** that happened during the period of time in question and write them down. These events can be projected milestones or other types of events that they noticed.

> *"The first this we need to do is to populate our timeline with important events that happened in the last sprint. Think about the last sprint and write down anything that stand out for you.*
>
> *Not all of the events will be related to the work that we did, there might be other important things that happened. For example, a team member getting sick, a new person joining, a broken build, a successful collaboration with another team, an announcement of organizational changes by the CEO, social team event, build breaking.*
>
> *Write each event on a separate sticky note."*

3. **Invite the team to share what they wrote and place their sticky notes** on the timeline together in chronological order. Let them figure out in what order the events happened – this will spark some discussions between team members already.

> *"Now that everyone has written down various events, I would like to ask the whole team to come to the board together to place the notes on our timeline. Look at each other notes and figure out the right sequence of events. Having a discussion here is key, so please do not put your notes up in a silo. Let's agree on what exactly happened in the last sprint. And if you remembered another important event, just add another note to the board."*

4. **Add new criteria to the timeline: write the word 'Impact'** to the left and say that each event has impacted us in some way. Write 'Positive' 20-30 cm above and 'Negative' 20-30 cm below the timeline line. Ask the team to distribute the events according to their impact: the stronger the impact, the higher or lower the card should be on the board. Some events might be grouped together.

> *"Now we need to analyze all the events that we have put on the board and move them up or down depending on how they impacted our sprint work. Was the impact positive or negative? How strong was the impact? Did it help us get things done faster or did it slow us down?*
>
> *Go back to the board and discuss together where each event belongs on the vertical axis. Make sure there is a general agreement. You should also think of whether some events can be grouped."*

5. **When the board is ordered chronologically and by impact, draw a line** connecting events to see a diagram of impact. You would expect it to have big fluctuations at the beginning and very short ones at the end since we have less uncertainty.

> *"With all the events placed on the timeline based on their impact, we can now see what was the general trend during our sprint. Here I will trace a line between events chronologically and we will see the fluctuations in the impact that happened during the sprint.*
>
> *It is absolutely ok to have big fluctuations at the start because we have more unknown, but if we see many big fluctuations at the end, it is a red flag for us because this is what would be putting our sprint in jeopardy. What pattern do you see now? What can you say about our sprint looking at the impact line?"*

6. **Identify what events you want to discuss**: first, circle those events that made the biggest impact (positive or negative); then ask the team what events they want to discuss first, if there are too many.

> *"Let's circle the events the made the biggest impact, whether positive or negative. Which one would you like to focus on first? I suggest we discuss at least one positive event before we move on to the negative ones."*

7. **Lead team discussion about each event**. The goal is to identify what can we do to repeat positive impact and avoid negative impact in the future iterations.

> *"It is time to really analyze the events that happened and the impact that they had. Firstly, we need to understand why this event was positive/negative. From the point of view of the team, how did this actually impact our work?*
>
> *All events happened for a reason. Let's discuss, what led to this event: was it something that happened outside of the team or was it something that we did ourselves?*
>
> *Now that we know more about this event and its impact, what can we do in the future based on what we learned? What steps should we take going forward to help us? Let's be very specific about the action items we would like to take into the next sprint."*

8. **In the previous step, you should have identified a variety of action items**. Help the team to choose which ones to focus on and ask for volunteers to drive them.

9. **Close the session** highlighting the fact that being able to analyze the events in the past in terms of their impact on the team's progress helps you identify how to address them in the future.

> *"In today's session, we were able to look at everything that happened in the last sprint in more details which allowed us to uncover how various events impact our work - this is something that we do not review often. It gave us great insights into how to get ready for those events in the future sprints and use what we learned to be more effective going forward."*

FACILITATOR NOTES

The best thing is to have a couple of events prepared by the facilitator in advance. It is sometimes difficult to remember important events right away, and some hints to what happened will help the team.

MANIFESTO

Identify the imbalances between Agile values versus traditional values.

DESCRIPTION

This technique is a great follow up on what really matters in an agile team for team members that have been working together for some and who have some understanding of agile and Scrum values and principles.

Using this technique will allow your team to get back to the basics and define what areas they should be focusing their improvement efforts on.

During the session, the four Agile value statements are used to brainstorm ideas around each part of each statement and see which values prevail in your team or through actions and practices. It is much less specific than other techniques, that is why it is best to do with an established team where there is no fear to bring up ideas that might be too vague.

Duration:	Facilitation difficulty:	Team maturity:
●●●○○	●●○	●●○○

WHITEBOARD SETUP

99

INSTRUCTIONS

1. **Introduce the technique** by referring to the Agile manifesto.

> *"Agile values are the baseline for all frameworks currently used by Agile teams whether we decide to use Scrum, Kanban or anything else. It is important to review these values and principles once in a while, to remind us what we should really focus on in order to become more Agile as we often get lost in processes and practices over time. In today's session, we will look into our ways of work and will analyze them through the prism of Agile Manifesto."*

2. **Ask the team to look back at the last sprint** or release and think about activities they were performing in relation to the categories identified by the Agile Manifesto. Ask them to write each activity on a separate sticky note.

> *"We will take each statement from the Agile Manifesto, and will consider each part of that statement a category. For example, 'individuals and interactions' is one category, and 'processes and tools' is another one, and so on.*
>
> *Now looking back at our past sprint, think about all the different activities we performed in relation to each category. I am going to give you a very simplified example. When we need help from another team, we might follow a specific process by creating a ticket in their system and awaiting their response - in this case, we are using 'processes and tools'. Or we might have gone to talk to them and collaborate on resolving the issue, prior to following a process, or after it. In this case, we are following 'individuals and interactions' value. This example is very simplistic, but I hope it gives you some idea of how to think in terms of the Agile Manifesto values."*

3. **Ask the team to put their notes on the board**, when the brainstorming part of the session is completed. Each activity can be related to only one value out of four and either one the right side, or on

the left. It's better if each team member reads each note out loud before placing it. It may spark some interesting discussions in the team when the decision is to be made where to place the note.

"It is time to put all our notes on the board in a relevant category. Please bring your notes and read them out loud before placing so that we all can agree on what category it fits the most. Each note will have to go in one value statement and either right or left side. If you are not sure where to put your note, we will need to decide as a team.

Once all the notes are up, we will be able to see the patterns in regards to the values."

4. **Analyze the distribution of the notes on the board.** Highlight where you see the most notes. Discuss with the team that you would expect to see the most activities on the left side (Agile values) but would still want to see some activities on the right side - we don't want to eliminate them completely.

"What can you see on the board? It is important for us to understand the patterns we see. Do any particular values prevail? Does it lean more towards Agile values on the left or traditional values on the right? Are there any values that are not populated at all? Are there any imbalances that you see?

Remember that we would like to be more Agile, so have most activities on the left side. At the same time, we still want to see some notes on the right side. As the Agile Manifesto states: while there is value in the items on the right, we value the items on the left more"

5. **Discuss with the team how to address imbalances in your Agile values** and what can be done to become more Agile next sprint without compromising the values on the right. This discussion should lead to some action items the team would like to take into the next sprint.

> *"Now that we have identified some imbalances in the way we approach our work, let's think about how we can address them. We need to think of the ways to exhibit more values on the left side without losing values on the right side. Some specific action items are in place.*
>
> *Firstly, what specific Agile values do we want to focus on in the next sprint? Secondly, what would be the first step for us to put more energy into this value?"*

6. **Ask for volunteers to drive the action items.**

7. **Close the session** by reminding what really matters in our work as an agile team is agile values and principles.

> *"In today's session, we had a chance to go to the roots of being agile - the Agile Manifesto. It was a great level re-setting exercise. We were able to identify all various activities we perform as a team without even thinking through the lens of agile values. With the knowledge about how our regular work is aligned with these values, we are able to refocus it on what really matters to an agile team like ours."*

MODIFICATIONS

The 12 Principles

Get more in-depth discussion by adding the twelve principles of Agile software development and ask the team to evaluate each one of them on the scale from '0' to '5' where '5' is 'following the principle in 100% of situations'. Discuss the gaps.

1. Customer satisfaction through early and continuous delivery of valuable software.
2. Welcome changing requirements, even late in development.
3. Working software is delivered frequently.

4. Close, daily cooperation between business people and developers.
5. Projects built around motivated individuals who are trusted.
6. Face-to-face conversation.
7. Working software is the primary measure of progress.
8. Sustainable development able to maintain constant pace.
9. Continuous attention to technical excellence and good design.
10. Striving for simplicity, minimizing waste and building efficient and fit for the purpose products.
11. Self-organizing teams, no roles or titles are promoted.
12. Continuous improvement with regular inspection and adaptation cycle.

FACILITATOR NOTES

Your team might focus on finding items for each category at first just to make sure everything is filled in. If you suspect something like this might happen, talk briefly about Agile values, but do not display them on the board until after the brainstorming session is over. This way your team will be thinking about activities to bring up in general terms, rather than in relation to specific categories.

THREE CIRCLES

See what challenges and concerns the team has control of or can influence.

DESCRIPTION

This technique is based on the Circle of Control, Circle of Influence and Circle of Concern approach to analyzing challenges one is facing. It helps the team to identify what concerns they can address and what concerns should be left on their own. It will help team members realize where they should spend most of their efforts when trying to solve various challenges.

Since this technique is heavily focused on issues, it is important to allow the team to recognize positive things that happened.

This can be a good exercise to do when a lot of issues keep coming back without ever being resolved as through this exercise the team might find out that those issues are out of their control.

Duration:	Facilitation difficulty:	Team maturity:
●●●○○	●●○	●●●○

WHITEBOARD SETUP

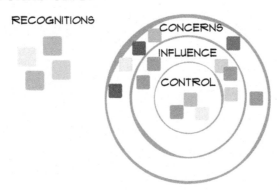

Concept:

The idea first appeared in The 7 Habits of Highly Effective People by Stephen R. Covey.

INSTRUCTIONS

1. **Introduce the technique** by talking about the importance of focusing your efforts on what matters.

> *"There are often multiple areas that we would like to improve upon and in order to succeed in our continuous improvement, we need to focus on the most important ones. It might be difficult to prioritize, so in today's session, we will use a technique that will help us with it. We will be looking at areas of improvement through the lens of our influence and control."*

2. **Ask the team to think about what have we achieved in the last sprint** and recognize someone or something for these achievements. Ask everyone to write notes for the Recognition Wall.

> *"Before we jump into discussing issues for the rest of the session, I would like us to spend some time to recognize each other for the good things that happened in the last sprint. Please spend a couple of minutes writing down who you would like to thank and what made your day in the last sprint. Then place them on the Recognition Wall.."*

3. **Ask the team to put their notes on the Recognition Wall** and read their notes out-loud. If it is appropriate in your situation, encourage the team to have a round of applause when the Recognition Wall is complete with everyone's notes.

> *"As you put the notes on the board, please read them out loud, especially, if they recognize someone on the team. Let's make sure we spend just enough time to look at the positive things that happened the last sprint."*

4. **Switch the discussion to the concerns the team has** after celebrating their accomplishments. Draw a big circle around the 'Concerns' title you wrote earlier and ask everyone to think about any concerns or challenges they are facing right now or face during the past sprint that has not been resolved yet.

> *"Now that we have looked at all the positive things that happened and celebrated them together, let's move on to the next part of this session: our concerns. We'll spend some time populating this circle: the circle of concerns. Think about all the concerns you have and the challenges we are facing as a team, specifically things that happened during the last sprint and things that have not been resolved so far. Please write each item on a separate sticky note."*

5. **Put all sticky notes inside the Circle of Concerns** and read them out loud. Group notes if relevant. Make sure the whole team agrees on what these concerns are related to.

> *"I will read all notes so that everyone has a general idea of what all of the concerns are. If you see items that are related to each other, let's group them together. And if you are not sure what an item is related to, raise it so that we can discuss and agree."*

6. **Draw a small circle in the middle and write 'Circle of Control' inside of it.** Ask the team what in the Circle of Concerns are directly in the team's control or could be in the team's control. Put all the notes that the team feels is in their control inside the small circle.

> *"We have identified all of our concerns and challenges. Let's see which items are actually in our control. Generally, it is the smallest amount, therefore, I have drawn a small circle in the middle. This is the circle of control.*
>
> *Let's review each item or group of items and decide whether it should go into the circle of control. Here is a couple of examples of what is typically in our control: our thoughts, our reactions to what is happening around us and our actions. Ask yourself this question: is it something that the team can resolve themselves?"*

7. **Discuss with the team what needs to be done to resolve the concerns in our Circle of Control** and what areas do we want to focus on. While we might have a lot of items in our control, we might not want to work on all of them at the same time. Create specific action items and ask for volunteers to drive them.

> *"Now that we know what concerns and challenges are actually in our control, let's immediately think about what we need to do to resolve them? If you feel there are too many items, we should agree on a subset of things we want to focus on right away.*
>
> *If you feel that something does not belong in the circle fo control because in reality there is nothing we can do about it, let's discuss once again whether we correctly placed the notes in the circle of control. But generally, since we placed these items here, there is got to be something that we can do about it."*

8. **Draw another circle in between the big and the small one and name it Circle of Influence**. Explain that some concerns that are not directly in our control can be moved into the Circle of Influence if we are ready to put some effort into them. Generally, those are things that we cannot control per se but can impact the outcome of.

"Here I am drawing another circle, a bit bigger than the Circle of Control. This is the Circle of Influence and we fully decide what we want to put into this circle. Let me explain.

Some of our concerns are out of our control, but we can still have an influence over them if we choose to do so. For example, I might be worried about our company producing too much waste with coffee cups. It's out of my control since there are a lot of people involved.

I can decide to put it into my Circle of Influence by, firstly, stop using paper cups at work, and then start advocating for banning paper cups with the HR and my colleagues. I can start a campaign to encourage people to bring reusable mugs to work or convince management to buy reusable mugs for the whole office.

I will be able to have some influence on the matter, but I will never be able to control it or what other people do. It is up to me to decide how much effort I want to put into moving a concern into my Circle of Influence."

9. **Ask the team to decide what concerns to move into the Circle of Influence** and what specific action items they would like to undertake next sprint to influence these items. Warn them to stay focused on just a handful of action items to not spread their efforts too thin. Ask for volunteers for actions.

"Circle of Influence is fully populated by us because it is our conscious decision to put effort into influencing these concerns. Think about what items that are still in the Circle of Concern would we want to put into our Circle of Influence as a team. Also, think about how much effort we want to put into resolving those items. We don't have to put all our time into it since we know these items are out of our control. We can just run small experiments to see whether our influence is strong enough to change something. If you feel overwhelmed, think of the smallest action we can take next sprint to start resolving this concern."

10. **Look at what is left in the Circle of Concerns.** Explain to the team that it is important to recognize that we have decided to not focus our efforts on resolving these concerns right now, therefore, we should leave them be and not try to solve them.

> *"Let's review everything that is left in the Circle of Concern. We have identified that all these items are out of our control and we are not ready to put extra effort in influencing them. It means that we should stop worrying about that. We can plan around these concerns and just be aware that these concerns are there, but we cannot let ourselves be side-tracked by them. Let's agree to put these things aside for at least a sprint and review if necessary."*

11. **Close the session** by recognizing that understanding our level of influence and control over various concerns helps us focus our efforts on what is really important.

> *"In today's session, we were able to understand what lies in our control, what we can influence and what is just a concern that cannot be addressed at the time. It will help us save our energy on more important things going forward and will take the focus away from the things that we can do nothing about. Let's always keep this in mind when we face new challenges going forward."*

FACILITATOR NOTES

As you describe different circles, remember to highlight the difference between the Circle of Control and the Circle of Influence as they often get mixed up. It's important to recognize that only person's own actions, thoughts and reactions are under control of this person. Everything else will most likely fall into the Circle of Concern or Influence.

At the same time pay attention to the number of items the team wants to bring into the Circle of Influence. Remind them that doing a poor job on many items is less valuable than doing a great job on just one.

CONTRADICTIONS

Find contradictions in what we want to be and what we actually do.

DESCRIPTION

This technique focuses on identifying inconsistencies in your processes, some things that contradict each other in the way we do things. Depending on your team dynamics, this can be a good intervention technique for your team to realize where they can improve. It can also be a good way to relax and have a laugh about how silly things often turn out. However, pay attention to your team dynamics as some people might take it as a reprimand.

This technique is used in facilitating many different workshops, including PSM II class, and is a great way to bring fun to your retrospective, while still focusing on solutions.

Duration:	Facilitation difficulty:	Team maturity:
●○○○○	●●○	●●●○

WHITEBOARD SETUP

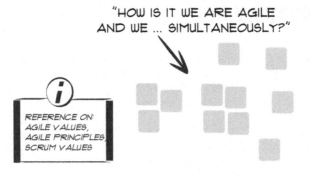

111

Concept:

ScrumButs are reasons why teams can't take full advantage of Scrum to solve their problems and realize the full benefits of product development using Scrum: https://www.scrum.org/resources/what-scrumbut.

Wicked Questions from Liberating Structures: http://www.liberatingstructures.com/4-wicked-questions/.

INSTRUCTIONS

1. **Start the session** by pointing at the whiteboard and explaining the technique.

> *"Sometimes we do certain things that might contradict each other. It is not something we do on purpose, but it is more related to the fact that we do not realize it until we stop to review our actions. In today's session, we will look at some contradictions to agile values and principles in a lightweight way and will find solutions to improve going forward."*

2. **Review the Agile and Scrum statements** to make sure everyone is on the same page.

> *"I wrote some references for us to think about on the whiteboard for Agile principles and Scrum values. When we talk about Agile or Scrum, it's important to get aligned on what we mean by it. Let's briefly review to make sure everyone understands what they mean. Are there any question in regards to these?"*

3. **Ask the team to fill in the blank in your contradictory statement** based on the Agile and Scrum reference. Allow 5-7 minutes for this exercise. Ideas can be written on sticky notes that you will later collect, or directly on the whiteboard if you have enough space.

> *"In the next step, we will use Agile principles and Scrum values that are written on the board as our guideline. We will need to fill in the blank in the statement 'How come we are agile and we are blank simultaneously?' Think about anything that might be contradictory to the agile and Scrum statements. It can be related to anything: people, processes, technology, maybe even the way our office space is organized.*
>
> *For example, how come we are agile and we have not delivered a working software in a couple of sprints? Or, how come we follow Scrum and we do not have a definition of "Done"?"*

4. **Put the notes on the board and read them out loud** allowing everyone to agree or disagree with the statements. At this stage, it is important to reach a consensus with the team. It is also an opportunity to group the notes together if they are similar or if they are related to the same topic.

> *"Put all of your notes to the board. As I read each note we'll try to group them where possible. If you disagree with a statement that was put on the board by someone else, let's discuss it right away and agree on whether it should be on the board. Remember, that this exercise is not to disregard the good work we were doing, but simply to understand how we can improve. Take it as an opportunity to review our ways of work."*

5. **Discuss what are the potential reasons and solutions for each contradiction.** Start with the biggest group - this most likely is the most pressing topic for the team.

> "Let's review the biggest group of notes as it seems to be the biggest contradiction. Then we'll move on to other notes and we'll cover as many as the time allows.
>
> Why do we think this statement is a contradiction? What are the underlying reasons for this? Since it is something that does not support Agile or Scrum principles, we should know why this happened. It can be something in or out of our control too. Is it something that we would like to solve?
>
> If the answer is yes, how would we like to address it? What can we do to make a positive change in the way we work? It can be a small action we take next sprint, as long as we agree to improve in this area."

6. **Choose a handful of items to address in the next sprint**, especially, if there are too many ideas and ask for volunteers.

7. **Ask the team's permission to compile the list of contradictions** to display in the team area of the team wiki page to hold each other accountable for resolving them. Explain to the team that you should come back to this list often to make sure you are making progress.

> "The list of contradictions that we have come up with is a great way to hold each other accountable in the future. We should be sure to review it often. My suggestion would be to collect this into a list and put it up on our team page or even display in the team area if we feel comfortable doing so. It will be a great motivator and a promise to others to improve. It may also help other teams start thinking about their ways of work in the same way"

8. **Close the session** by talking about how reviewing your actions helped you uncover hidden improvement opportunities.

> *"Sometimes we do things that contradict each other and the best way to solve this is to review your actions once in a while to make sure that you are still on track to reach your goals. We did a great job doing this in today's session. It is the first step in drastically improving our ways of work and becoming more agile."*

MODIFICATIONS

Team agreements

You can switch the focus of the session on specific team agreements instead of Agile and Scrum in general. In this case, for reference write or display your team working agreements, maybe even the definition of done.

You can also allow team members to pick and choose the first part of the phrase from the reference statements, for example, "How is it that our Definition of Done includes 80% unit test coverage BUT our latest build has only 60% coverage?"

FACILITATOR NOTES

Be prepared to have some discussions around certain contradictions to not be related to the reference. Some of the things we do have a non-direct impact on the Agile values and principles and it might be difficult to see how they are related. You should be able to connect the dots if the team is not clear on some of them.

It is recommended to use Agile principles as described in the official website for the Agile Manifesto: http://agilemanifesto.org/principles.html

In relation to Scrum, you can take some introductory statements from the Scrum Guide as well as the elements of Scrum, for example:

- Significant aspects of the process must be visible to those responsible for the outcome.
- People personally commit to achieving the goals of the Scrum Team.

- The Scrum Team members have the courage to do the right thing and work on tough problems.
- Everyone focuses on the work of the Sprint and the goals of the Scrum Team.
- The Scrum Team and its stakeholders agree to be open about all the work and the challenges with performing the work.
- Scrum Team members respect each other to be capable, independent people.
- The Scrum Team uses a previously agreed upon definition of "Done" to assess when work is complete on the product Increment; etc.

5

DEMANDING FACILITATION TECHNIQUES

The techniques in this section of the book demand good facilitation skills as they open up a lot of discussion around a variety of topics.

It would be common for the team to get off track fairly quickly and you should be able to bring the focus back. Some of the techniques can also raise controversial subjects and challenging questions. Be prepared to facilitate it.

With these techniques, you will need additional preparation to run them properly. First of all, you should prepare some good examples to explain the concepts of the techniques.

LEARNING HABITS

Learn what activities bring you the best learning experience.

DESCRIPTION

This technique helps the teams focus on learnings from the previous sprint by dividing activities into successful ones or failed ones in terms of their outcomes, and mistakes, experiments or good practices in terms of the behaviour.

The underlying concept suggests that learning is optimal when we run experiments because we cannot know whether they would succeed or fail in advance, so we will learn something either way. At the same time, we don't usually learn anything by just repeating good or bad habits, unless they give us unexpected results.

It is a great opportunity for the team to focus their attention on learning.

This technique might be difficult to understand from the start, so you should be prepared to answer many different questions.

Duration:	Facilitation difficulty:	Team maturity:
●●●○○	●●●	●●●○

WHITEBOARD SETUP

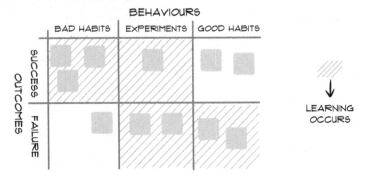

Concept:

Celebration grid from Management 3.0 2010-2018, www.management30.com.

INSTRUCTIONS

1. **Introduce the technique** by talking learning opportunities and the difference between behaviours and outcomes.

> *"In today's session, we will be looking at how we learn through our successes and failures as well different behaviours we have. Whatever the action we take, we usually expect it to either succeed or fail. This would be an outcome of our action. At the same time, each endeavour can be based on different behaviours. We generally either do something that proved to be a good practice, or we repeat a mistake hoping it works out, or we decide to experiment with something new. Depending on the chosen behaviour, you have different learning opportunities. You would always learn something new when experimenting, whether your experiment succeeds or fails. You usually won't learn much by repeating good practices or mistakes. The only time when you learn something new with those is if your mistake suddenly succeeds or your good practice fails."*

2. **Give some examples of behaviours and their learnings.** Use real-life examples for better understanding. You can adjust the ones given below.

"Let's take a simple example of going for a coffee.

I usually order tea, because I don't really like coffee. So when I order black tea, it's a good practice: it makes me feel energized and more productive. Whenever I order tea, I know the outcome, so I won't learn anything from it. But once I ordered tea and it was poor, so I was feeling nauseous afterwards. I learned that I shouldn't keep the tea bag in the water for too long. I learned because my good practice failed.

Now, since I usually don't like coffee, I know that ordering it is a mistake. But once I ordered a new type of espresso for a change and I actually liked it. I learned from this mistake that on some occasions coffee can be a good idea.

Going back to experiments, I decided to order matcha latte - something that I never tried before. Whatever the outcome is, I will learn something new from it about my coffee tastes."

3. **Ask the team to write down their activities from the last sprint.** Here they should not focus on what behaviours or outcomes those activities relate to. Ask the team to list out any actions that they would like to highlight regardless of the learnings.

"Let's look at our last sprint. For the next 5-7 minutes, think about all of the meaningful activities that you or the team undertaken in the last sprint. Only think of the activities themselves, not their outcomes and not the behaviours that they relate to. Whatever activity or action comes to your mind, write it down on a sticky note."

4. **Ask the team to come to the Learning Habits graph** and distribute the notes between behaviours and outcomes.

"Next let's put all the notes on the Learning Habits graph in the corresponding section. Do not think about learning just yet, only focus on the outcomes of these activities and what behaviours influenced them.

For the outcome, think about the following questions. What was the outcome of this action: did it work well? If yes, it was a success. Is it something they feel should be improved or stopped? If yes, it was a failure.

After that, think about which behaviour was the activity based on. Was it something that you knew would work well from previous experience? Then it was a good practice. Was it something that is known to bring negative results? Then it was a bad habit. Was it something new you have not tried before? Then it was an experiment."

5. **Give the team some time to review the graph together** once it is populated with everyone's notes. The team should focus on learnings from each activity or define if an activity did not bring any learnings.

"Review all of the notes of the graph as a team. Think of each activity in terms of learnings: were you able to learn something from it? In the next step of this exercise, we will be able to discuss each section of the graph together."

6. **Discuss each activity and learnings, starting from successful experiments**, then review failed experiments, then look at successful bad habits and failed good habits. You do not need to review bad habits that failed or good practices that succeeded since generally there are no learnings involved.

"Let's review the activities on the graph in more detail. You had a chance to think about what you learned from them - it will be a good input to the questions I will be asking now.

We will start with successful experiments. Think about why this was a success. What can we repeat from this success in the upcoming sprint?

Moving on to the failed experiments, let's think why this was a failure. What could have been done to prevent it from failing? Experiments always bring the most learning since it is something new. What other experiments we can run in the future?

Now let's look at bad habits that succeeded. What was the success factor that led to positive outcomes? How can we adapt our bad habit to make it a good one?

The last section we will review is good habits that failed. How come we failed to get the positive outcome of good practice? What went wrong and what have we learned that we can implement next time?"

7. **Compile all the action items that came out of the discussion** and ask for volunteers for each task the team decided to bring into the next sprint. If there are too many, ask the team to vote on the most important ones.

8. **Thank the team for participating and close the retrospective** by pointing out how important learning is, whether we succeed or fail..

"In today's session, we were able to put our focus on the learnings from our habits and experiments. The outcome of our action in itself is less important as long as we're able to learn something and implement it in the future. Thanks to this retrospective, we will be able to continuously improve based on the learnings we have discovered."

MODIFICATIONS

Futurespective

Use the Learning Behaviours chart to predict team's potential learnings in one week, one month or six months in the future. Focus on what learnings the team might get out of continuing the same good practices or mistakes, and what new experiments they can try to learn more.

FACILITATOR NOTES

During the brainstorming session, your team might start thinking of the activities that can be put into categories on the chart, instead of doing it after collecting their ideas. In this case, hiding the chart might help them focus on getting as many important activities as possible, before categorizing them.

Alternate the questions to help your team get more ideas about the learnings. For example: "What should we keep doing?", "What was unexpected?", "Were we surprised by the outcome?"

EXPERIMENTS

Define and prepare experiments the team can run next sprint.

DESCRIPTION

This technique focuses primarily on experiments and encourages the team to try something new in the next sprint. It is a good technique for a team with a high level of Agile maturity or in a situation when your team had a blast past few iterations and encountered low amounts of issues to resolve.

The exercises are designed to spark creativity in your team and get them excited about the next sprint. Because it focuses mainly on generating ideas and making a plan, the more ideas the team already had before the better. This technique would be a great opportunity to review the notes from your previous retrospectives and get back to solutions the team never got a chance to implement before.

Duration:	Facilitation difficulty:	Team maturity:
●●●○○	●●●	●●●●

WHITEBOARD SETUP

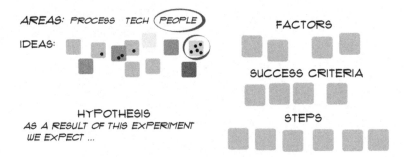

125

INSTRUCTIONS

1. **Start the session** by highlighting some positive things that happened during the past sprint that now allow you to experiment.

   > *"We had some successful sprints and were doing a fine job improving continuously. It means that we have more room for experiments in the upcoming sprints. So instead of focusing on the challenges we faced, during this session we will be designing a perfect experiment to run in the next sprint."*

2. **Help the team decide on the general topic of the experiment** by presenting three areas of potential experiments: process, technology or people. Give some examples of various experiments related to each area. Ask the team to choose one area out of three to focus on in this session - facilitate the discussion until the team reaches consensus.

   > *"Because we are planning for only one sprint, we should focus on a single experiment to run. For that, we should first decide what kind of experiment everyone would be excited about. As a team, we need to agree on the area first. We will be choosing from one of three: experiment related to our processes, to our technology or to people.*
   >
   > *For example, something related to processes can be a change we want to make to our support model. Something related to technology can be a use of a new integration with BitBucket. Something related to people can be a change in who we include in our Sprint Events.*
   >
   > *For now, we are only choosing an area in which we would like to run our experiment. Let's discuss or vote on the area we'll focus on for the rest of this session."*

3. **Run a brainstorming activity to find as many potential experiments as possible**. Set a timer for 5 minutes and ask everyone to shout out experiment ideas and write each one of them down on a whiteboard.

> *"Now that we have identified the area in which we would like to run an experiment, we need to brainstorm as many ideas as possible. There are no bad ideas, every idea can be taken into consideration. For the next five minutes give me ideas for experiments related to the area we chose as a team and I will write them down. We will not be discussing the ideas just yet, so only give experiment ideas, not your opinion about them. To make sure you don't set up boundaries for your ideas, answer this question: what could we do if there were zero constraints to the way we work?"*

4. **When the time is up, read through all the ideas listed and group similar ones**. Ask the team to vote on the ideas. You can use any voting technique that makes the most sense in your team setting. At the end of this exercise, the team needs to decide what experiment to run the next sprint.

> *"We have many great ideas. Let's see if we can group some of them.*
>
> *Now it is time to decide which one we'll be trying in the next sprint. We should focus on only one and put as much effort into as possible. Let's vote on the idea that you think we should focus on."*

5. **Take note (or a picture) of the rest of the experiments** for later reference - you don't want any distractions for the next part of the session.

> *"I will collect all of the other ideas that we did not choose and we might get back to them next time, whenever we have an opportunity to run more experiments. I will remove them from the board for the rest of the session so that we don't get distracted."*

6. **In the middle of the board write the short name of the chosen experiment**. Below write the first headline: Hypothesis. Ask the team to think about what we are trying to achieve with this experiment or

what is the problem this experiment is supposed to solve. This will be your hypothesis.

> *"We have a general idea of what the experiment going to be. Let's name our experiment. The next step for us is to define our hypothesis: what we are hoping to solve with the experiment. Let's write it down in the following way: as a result of this experiment, we expect to... This will be our hypothesis that we will be trying to prove, or disprove during the next sprint."*

7. **Write the next headline: Factors.** Ask the team to think about external and internal factors that need to be set up for this experiment to be executed correctly. Give some examples of what it can be. Write down the list as the team gives ideas.

> *"Now that we know what problem we are trying to solve, let's identify what we need to run our experiment successfully. Think about what we need to prepare, what support we would like to have from our management, other teams, or ourselves. Are there any tools or processes we need in place? What other assumptions are we making?"*

8. **Write the next headline: Success Criteria.** Ask the team to identify the success criteria for this experiment. This needs to be expressed as a SMART goal or several goals to help the team measure their progress.

> *"The next step in creating an experiment is to define success criteria for it. How do we know that we have proven our hypothesis? What is the minimum outcome? And what we would like to achieve ideally? ...*

> *The items here should be written in a form of SMART goals. For example, increase customer satisfaction by 10% thanks to the new support model. There is a specific measure in there, that we obviously will need to calculate before we start the experiment, it is achievable, relatable, short and tangible. All of the success criteria we put in here should be as specific."*

9. **Write the next headline: Steps.** This is a very important part of the exercise and you should allow enough time for it even if it is at the end of the session. Ask the team to plan their experiment in small steps that need to happen in order for the experiment to work. Remember that factors might need some pre-work to allow the experiment to happen. Encourage the team to think about specific action items that can be worked on and completed.

> *"Now that we have identified all the essential parts of our experiment, we need to think about our action plan. Let us decompose the experiment into clear steps that can be owned by a single team member. We can even split it up into days to make sure we are on track with our experiment during the sprint. The action items have to be very specific and clear to everyone on the team.*
>
> *Remember the factors we have previously identified and any metrics we need to collect - without these in place, our experiment is bound to be executed incorrectly. What do we need to do to make sure that we prepare for our experiment correctly?"*

10. **Ask for volunteers for each action items** and set timelines for them where possible.

11. **Close the retrospective** by congratulating the team on continuously striving to improve in the spirit of Agile and restating the goal of the experiment for the next sprint.

> *"In today's session, we were able to design an experiment that will help us continuously improve and try new things. We were also able to identify a very clear step-by-step plan to execute it which means that we have more chance to succeed with it. And no matter what, we will learn a lot after running this experiment."*

MODIFICATIONS

Multiple experiments

While this technique is focusing on a single experiment, it is possible to brainstorm and define several smaller experiments. If you feel that your team is coming up with ideas that can be executed in parallel or if your team is eager to try out more things, extend the session to plan several smaller experiments.

FACILITATOR NOTES

Keep the team focused on the definitions provided. While it is tempting for the team to delve into details of what is blocking them, help them get back on track and keep discussing the topics defined in the technique.

ANTI-ACTIONS

See if you perform any counter-intuitive actions that might lead you to failure.

DESCRIPTION

This technique gives the team an opportunity to look at their sprint goal from a completely different angle by asking them to come up with counter-intuitive solutions to make sure they fail. It can be a fun exercise to have with the team after a difficult sprint when the sprint goal was not met. This technique can reveal how some of our actions unintentionally might lead us to the results we do not want.

This is a fun exercise that helps bring joy in your regular retrospective and easily put the focus back on solving problems without the tension it sometimes creates. However, it does require strong facilitation to keep the team on point.

Duration:	Facilitation difficulty:	Team maturity:
●○○○○	●●●	●●●○

WHITEBOARD SETUP

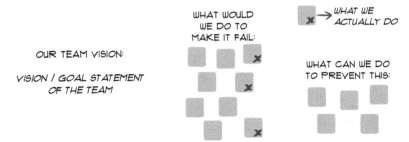

OUR TEAM VISION:

VISION / GOAL STATEMENT OF THE TEAM

WHAT WOULD WE DO TO MAKE IT FAIL:

✗ → WHAT WE ACTUALLY DO

WHAT CAN WE DO TO PREVENT THIS:

Concept:

TRIZ from Liberating Structures: http://www.liberatingstructures.com/6-making-space-with-triz/

INSTRUCTIONS

1. **Start the session** by explaining the technique. Read the goal you have written on the board out loud and verify that the team agrees with it. If needed, modify the goal statement.

> *"Have you ever wondered what would it take to make us fail? It's a weird question that we will be asking ourselves today in order to understand if we are doing any counter-intuitive actions ourselves.*
>
> *I have put our team vision/goal statement on the board as a starting point. This is what we strive for as a team. Does everyone agree with this statement? If not, let's make sure we get to an agreement before we jump into today's retrospective."*

2. **Ask the team to look at the goal and imagine to be team's worst competitor.** Ask them to write ideas of how to make sure that the team fails in achieving their goal or vision.

> *"Now that we have all agreed on our vision/goal, imagine that you are here to make sure it fails. Imagine you are a competing team or organization infiltrating our team as a spy. What would you do to sabotage the progress towards this goal, if you wanted this goal to be a complete and utter failure? What other things can go wrong to ensure this goal is not met? Think of everything that would be counter-productive, even if a little bit absurd. Be creative."*

3. **Give everyone some time to read and discuss the notes.** Tell the team that now is time to think critically about the anti-actions that they have identified: does anything look familiar. Allow enough time for analysis as this is a very important part of the exercise. Encourage

the team to take additional notes of actual anti-actions they are doing.

"We did a good job identifying all the terrible things we can do to make it fail. Now let's think critically about everything we wrote. Is there anything that we did the last sprint that resembles any of the anti-actions we have identified? Does anything at all sounds familiar? Have we ever observed similar behaviours? If yes, put a dot on the note, or write new notes if necessary.

Sometimes we do counterproductive actions without even realizing it, and it is just human nature. This is a time where we can finally figure it out. There is no judgment involved, it is just an opportunity to identify these counterproductive behaviours and improve them."

4.   **After identifying the team's anti-actions, ask them to think of a mitigation plan**. The first step is to understand why these counterproductive behaviours happen, then define what to do about them.

"As we have seen, without even realizing it, we are ourselves doing things that take us further away from our goal. Let's understand why this is happening. What are the underlying reasons for some of these activities? We can group them together based on that.

With a better understanding of why we do certain things, we can plan improvement actions. What can be done to help stop these unwanted activities and behaviours? Since now we know these actions are counterproductive, we should think of a way to improve our ways of work in order to get closer to our team goal/vision."

5.   **With some action items identified, ask them to decide which ones** they would like to implement in the next sprint and ask for volunteers on each action.

6.   **Close the session** by saying that as we now know what anti-actions can prevent us from achieving our next sprint goal, it will be easier to

recognize them and hence to counteract.

> "In today's session, we had a chance to analyze our actions and behaviours in a different light and understand whether we are doing something that goes against our goals. This will allow us to spot these type of behaviours going forward and adjust to be on track to meeting our goals."

MODIFICATIONS

Anti-goals

As the initial concept of TRIZ activity suggests, you can start by identifying the worst possible outcome that the team can achieve and proceed to identify anti-actions to achieve that anti-goal. This will turn the technique into a futurespective and can be an interesting switch from the technique definition as described above.

Anti-team dynamics

Another way to approach this technique is to take team agreements as your baseline and see what the team does that goes against it. It is a good way to review your team charter at the same time and can uncover behaviours that never went along with what the team agreed on.

FACILITATOR NOTES

It is important to keep the discussion around anti-actions separated from blaming actual people on the team. Since this exercise is aimed at exaggerating potential issues, you might need to jump in and help the team focus on the actions themselves rather than people performing them (most likely, without any ill intent).

QUESTION TIME

Allow each team member to ask open questions to each other and to you.

DESCRIPTION

This technique can help you level out conversations and let everyone on the team speak up and share their opinion. This technique might yield unexpected results with unexpected questions and answers. It is especially good when the team has a different level of participation, when everyone seems to have an idea but is having a hard time getting it out. This technique is better performed in a team with no or little conflicts because some team members might want to ask questions directed at each other. That is why strong facilitation is required. The teams also get excited about being able to ask questions to their Scrum Master which gives you an opportunity to share your opinions openly.

Duration: Facilitation difficulty: Team maturity:

●●●●●   ●●●   ●●●●

WHITEBOARD SETUP

RULES OF THE GAME

CHALLENGE CONCEPTS, NOT PEOPLE: QUESTIONS HAVE TO BE ON THE PROCESS

ONE PERSON ANSWERS: NO INTERRUPTIONS

ONE TIME = ONE QUESTION: NO PROBING QUESTIONS

OPEN QUESTIONS ONLY: NO "YES" OR "NO" QUESTIONS

SAME QUESTION ALLOWED, IF ASKED TO SOMEONE NEW.

Concept:

Activity: Circle of Questions from Agile Retrospectives by Ken Schwaber, Diana Larsen, Esther Derby

INSTRUCTIONS

1. **When everyone is already sitting down, introduce the technique** to your team. You want the team to sit down first in random order to prevent them from choosing their questions partner.

> *"Today we will have a forum of questions and answers that will help us the most important topics to focus on. This will be a chance for everyone to speak up and ask the most important questions to each other. Your question and answer partners will be on your right and on your left."*

2. **Make an emphasis on the rules**. Go over each one of them and let the team know that you will be monitoring these rules with vigour. You want to make sure that everyone feels safe and knows they can rely on you.

> *"Before we start, we should understand the rules for today's session. It is extremely important as it this the way we ensure we create a safe environment for each other to ask and answer questions without judgement. Remember the retrospective prime directive: regardless of what we discover, we understand and truly believe that everyone did the best job they could, given what they knew at the time, their skills and abilities, the resources available, and the situation at hand.*
>
> *We are here to ask questions about the ways we work, not specific people. Each person will have a chance to ask a question and to answer a question, without interruptions. Only open questions are allowed, and only one question is allowed per round.*
>
> *I will be monitoring these rules during the session. Let's make sure we make this session as productive as possible."*

3. **Allow the team 3 minutes to gather their thoughts** and write down some questions they would like to ask. Everyone should have an opportunity to ask and answer two questions.

> *"Let's spend a couple of minutes to think about questions you would like to ask. Consider who you are sitting next to - those will be the people you will asking questions. Write down some question ideas if needed."*

4. **Ask the first question to the person on your right**. The easiest way to go around the table is to start with yourself, then continue the direction of questions until the last person asks a question to you. After you answer, ask the question back to the person on your left and continue the circle until it gets back to you.

> *"I will start the circle of questions. Then we'll go around the table until the question gets back to me, and then we'll start in another direction. Remember the rules when asking questions.*
>
> *Try to give as much information in your answer as possible, don't just cut it short, or we won't get enough details to have an engaging discussion afterwards. Once you finished answering the question, ask your question to the next person in the circle and so on."*

5. **After two rounds, conclude on the most common questions**, if anything was asked more than once, or vote on two or three questions to focus on.

> *"With two rounds worth of questions we have enough information to continue our discussion in more detail. Let's look at all the different questions we have. Which ones were the most common? Do you see any patterns?*
>
> *We won't be able to deep dive in all of the questions, so let's decide what we want to focus on. Would you like to give you votes for the question-answer that seems to be the most important to you?"*

6. **Focus the discussion on solutions and action items**. If you captured some of the action ideas during the questions, review with the team whether this is something you would like to focus on in the next sprint.

> *"Let's review the questions and answers we have chosen in the lens of solutions and action items. Why is this question important to us? Is there a concern that we would like to address? What can we do to get a better answer to the question or resolve a concern we have?*
>
> *Our goal in this part is to think of what we would like to focus on doing the next sprint based on the questions and answers we got."*

7. **Close the retrospective** by thanking the team for being open to ask and answer questions from each other.

> *"Today's session was a great opportunity to hear each other's unbiased opinions that helped us uncover more interesting topics and let every single team member express themselves. We should keep the same spirit of asking and answering questions to each other in our daily work as a team as well to allow open discussions and continuous improvement to happen outside of our retrospectives."*

MODIFICATIONS

Topic defined

As a way to make the questions more specific, you might want to define a topic for the session. It can be related to something that happened during a sprint, or a general improvement area you would like to cover.

FACILITATOR NOTES

Every time I run this technique, the team asks me what I think about how they are doing, so be ready for this and prepare a good answer, especially, if there is a specific topic you wanted to cover.

Creating safe environment here is key. If you are not sure that your team has positive dynamics, refrain from using this technique, or make the questions more pointed. For example, prepare some sample questions ready to give as examples to the team. In addition, you can use a "talking stick" to avoid interruptions.

Don't spend too much time managing the questions: it's ok to have some people ask funny questions as they can help everyone feel more comfortable.

This technique takes quite a lot of time. To make sure you get to solutions, allow more time than for a usual retrospective. If you don't allocate enough time, the discussion will end with just questions and no action items.

Here are some sample questions to use:

- What is currently our team's biggest pain point?
- How well do you think we do X? (e.g. estimates, planning, task sharing, etc.)
- What our team is missing to be a top performer?
- What puzzles us?
- What do you think we do best?
- If someone from outside was describing us, what would they say?
- How do we want to be perceived?
- How do you think you are perceived?
- How are you defining commitment?
- Are you collaborating or negotiating with your customer?
- Do we have time to address technical debt?

VALUE TREE

Align your team's values and characteristics with values and characteristics of High Performing teams.

DESCRIPTION

This technique was initially created for coaching agile teams on values of agile development. It is also a great tool to realign your team on the values and define areas of improvement to achieve higher performance in a long term.

As part of a retrospective it is an opportunity for the team to look closer in the ways they are working through the lens of a high-performing agile team. It can help some teams understand better what you are trying to achieve as a Scrum Master of their team and adjust their behaviours to be more agile.

Duration:	Facilitation difficulty:	Team maturity:
●●●●○	●●●	●●○○

Concept:

Chapter 2 from Coaching Agile Teams by Lyssa Adkins

WHITEBOARD SETUP

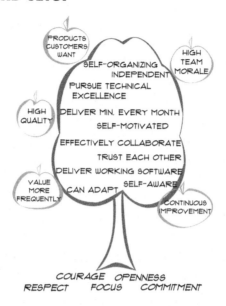

INSTRUCTIONS

1. **Introduce the technique to the team** by briefly talking about building high-performing teams as an concept of Agile.

> *"Today we will be reviewing Agile we are as a team through the lens of a high-performing team values, characteristics and outcomes, because one of the positive changes that Agile brings to organization is creation of high-performing teams. To helps us understand this better I will be using a tree metaphor. It will all come together as I start explaining to you different parts of this metaphor."*

2. **Describe the roots of your tree as Scrum values.** Talk about how values become a foundation for your team and define how the team grows going forward.

> "There are five Scrum values that create a foundation for a high-performing team. These values are our roots: commitment, courage, focus, openness and respect. What it means on a daily basis is this:
>
> Each team member personally commits to achieving the goals of the team versus individual goals. The team members have courage to do the right thing and work on tough problems instead of avoiding them or instead of working on something that doesn't matter. Everyone focuses on the work decided by the team, not something on the side or coming from outside of the team. The team and its stakeholders agree to be open about all the work and the challenges with performing the work. The team members respect each other's knowledge and skills and value each other's opinions even if they disagree."

3. **Explain how strong roots would transform into characteristics of your team**. These will be the leaves of high performing tree. Go through the sticky notes with characteristics you prepared earlier and put them up on your tree.

> "If our values, hence our roots, are strong, then our team tree will be growing well and will sprout leaves. Our leaves are our team characteristics, the characteristics of a highly agile team. The more leaves our tree has, the more agile our team is and the more light it can gather. As a team with strong values, we will become self-organizing and independent. We will be able to effectively collaborate because we trust each other. We will be able to adapt and adjust our ways of work thanks to high self-awareness. We will be able to pursue technical excellence while still delivering working software every sprint.
>
> All these are characteristics of a high performing team."

4. Describe what results would strong values and strong team characteristics bring. Go through the sticky notes with results of a high performing team you prepared earlier and put them up on your tree.

"As our tree gets more sunlight from the abundant leaves it has it starts to grow fruits - results that a highly agile team brings. With strong values and strong characteristics we know we can achieve much more. We will have high-team morale. We will be able to deliver products that customer actually want, and we'll be able to deliver them more frequently. Our products will have high quality, and we will be able to continuously improve. These are the results we strive for when we think about a high-performing team."

5. Ask the team to think deeply about what they are missing on their team tree: values, characteristics, results.

"Now that we understand how a high-performing team grows, let's think critically about our team. Are we a highly agile team? Where can we actually improve.

Think deeply about these questions: Where are our roots weak? What leaves do we want to work on? What fruits have a stale taste?"

6. Go around the room giving each person a couple of minutes to answer the three questions. Time it, if necessary. Write down ideas as people speak.

"Let's make sure everyone has an opportunity to speak. I will go around the room and will ask each person the three questions. Please answer openly what you think about how our team is doing ad we will discuss in more details afterwards. If you already have some ideas for how to solve the misalignment, please also talk about that during your turn."

7. **As you identified the most important areas of improvement**, go into a discussion about what can be done with the whole group. Write down the action items and volunteers to drive them.

> *"We should focus on how we can become more Agile and move closer to becoming a high-performing team. With some areas of improvement identified, let's focus on finding solutions and specific actions items we would like to work on in the next sprint."*

8. **Close the retrospective** by reminding the team that if we want to be agile, we should always remember the values of agile and what we want to achieve as an agile team.

> *"In today's session we had a chance to level-set what being a highly agile team really means in terms of values, characteristics and expected results. It was a great exercise that helped us understand how to improve and move in the right direction to real agility."*

MODIFICATIONS

Other framework values

This technique can be adapted to any kind of framework and team dynamics your would like to focus on. Setting a different foundation for you Agile tree will still yield the same characteristics and results of a high-performing team. At the same time, you are free to choose what you would like to put on the tree as leaves and fruits.

For example, for DevOps use the following roots: Work lean, Embrace failure, Automate everything, Demand diversity, Driving a culture change.

FACILITATOR NOTES

Prepare your presentation in advance to have an easy flowing talk about values, team characteristics and outcomes as it will help the team understand how it all ties back to the tree metaphor. It is good to have specific examples, especially, in relation to values.

Allow enough time for this technique and timebox your explanation at the beginning.

6

ENDNOTES

For me personally, retrospective is the most important part of Scrum Master's work with an agile team. It is a time that really helps the team to come together, build trust and understand how they can improve. Inspection and adaptation is a crucial part of building agile teams.

This book covers twenty techniques that can be used in many different situations, but it doesn't have to stop there. With modification provided in the book, you can create many more retrospective techniques to run with your teams.

Continue to evolve your retrospectives once you have experience with running them. Look for ideas in other fields, good approaches to coaching and asking questions, workshops for team building and other ways to engage your team. The only thing you need to keep in mind are the steps to run any retrospective that I covered in chapter 1.

While some teams might be resistant to trying different retrospective techniques because they think it is too touchy-feely, remember, as a Scrum Master you are in charge of a process and you should be free to change the way you facilitate team retrospectives.

Moreover, I have not encountered a single team who disliked using different retrospective techniques once they tried them out. Changing techniques will bring more focus to the discussions and engagement from the team.

By introducing new techniques to your regular retrospectives you will show the team that experimenting and trying new things is a good practice and they will naturally start doing it in their daily work.

And whatever you do in your retrospectives, remember that change is hard, and every single step in the right direction matters.

KEY TAKEAWAYS

This book contains so much advice that can be used in a variety of situations. There is a small list of things I would like you to remember from this book if you were to forget everything else:

Experiment.

Look for new ways to approach things. It is only by trying new things you will succeed.

I had uninspiring debates with some agile practitioners who believed that everything has to follow a set of guidelines and there is no other way to do thing.

It saddens me to see that approach to agile sometimes. Look at this book as an opportunity to experiment not only with your retrospectives, but with other elements of agile and Scrum, or Kanban, or any other framework you are following.

Be ready to fail.

During the years of working with many agile (and not very) teams, I have seen failure. It is tough. Even with things that were proven to work, you might fail.

Techniques in this book work, but there are so many different factors that might lead them to failure. Never give up, keep trying in different situations, different sprints, different teams.

Learn from each of your experiments, successful or failed, and adjust the way you facilitate your retrospectives, planning, daily scrum, or any other event you might happen to have.

Celebrate small wins with your team, and just have fun!

We spend so much time with our teams as Scrum Masters (at least, I really hope you do), that we can't let this time be unpleasant. Become fully a part of your agile team by bringing positive and fun discussions into your retrospectives.

ACKNOWLEDGEMENTS

I have drawn my inspiration from many different sources and I would like to give the proper credit to every person, book and article that inspired me to write this book.

I could have never done this without my great Scrum Master team at Bluecat Networks back in 2016, led by Matthew Grierson. Together with Matt and Christopher Beaudoin, we were able to kick start the initial idea of using different retrospective techniques with our Scrum teams. Big thank you to them for their dedication, co-creation and simple awesomeness.

I would like to say a special thank you for all the backers of my Indiegogo campaign for the Retrospective Poker cards. Their contributions allowed me to focus on the book as a follow up to the campaign. You can read more about the campaign here:

https://www.indiegogo.com/projects/retrospective-poker-cards-for-scrum-masters/

Each retrospective technique in this book is unique, however, my inspiration has been drawn from many of these resources:

- Agile Retrospectives by Esther Derby, Diana Larsen and Ken Schwaber
- Liberating Structures (http://www.liberatingstructures.com/)
- Coaching Agile Teams by Lyssa Adkins (https://www.infoq.com/articles/adkins-coaching-agile-teams-chapter2)
- Seven Habits of Highly Effective People by Stephen Covey
- The Coaching Habit: Say Less, Ask More & Change the Way Your Lead Forever Paperback by Michael Bungay Stanier
- Management 3.0 (https://management30.com/)

- Agile Manifesto & Scrum Guide
- Fun Retrospectives website (http://www.funretrospectives.com/)
- Spotify retrospective ideas

I would also like to thank the agile teams I worked with who allowed me to run experiments in their retrospectives, for better or worse. It gave me opportunities to test and improve on my ideas.

ALWAYS MORE TO COME

This book is one of many ideas I have to help Scrum Masters around the world coach their agile teams. I think that the more tools and practices we can share, the better the industry will be able to challenge the status quo and continuously improve.

We spend so much time at work that we can't afford to live those days unhappy, doing boring and unsatisfactory work. With great change agents and coaches, the workplaces can be transformed to nurture self-motivated, self-organizing teams who build products that customers love.

If you want to learn more about what I do, head to www.scrummastered.com and sign up to my newsletter. I share practical tips and personal stories about the Scrum Master role, agile teams, coaching, mentoring and facilitation.

If you are also interested in getting a deck or Retrospective Poker cards, head down to http://www.scrummastered.com/retrospectives where I will be posting news about where to buy the cards.

Keep in touch with me on social media:

- LinkedIn: https://www.linkedin.com/in/dariabagina/
- Instagram: https://www.instagram.com/scrummastered/
- Twitter: https://twitter.com/daria_bagina

About the author

Daria became a Scrum Master in 2014 when the organization she was working for was going through an agile transformation. Thanks to the great mentors and colleagues in her professional life, she was able to quickly find her way and become successful in the Scrum Master role.

Daria worked with more than ten teams in less than 4 years, she got the needed experience and developed great tools to use in her daily job that led her to building strong teams in challenging environments.

Her main focus these past two years was agile retrospectives and helping growing other Scrum Masters in the field.

But what really matters is what her peers can tell you about her.

> *"Daria ardently works for her teams as a Scrum Master should - removing impediments, defending and compassionately coaching and challenging. She will passionately advocate on her team's behalf using Agile principles and values, while still being pragmatic about outcomes."*
>
> **-- Matthew Grierson, Agile & Lean Coach**

> *Daria is a strong communicator that is not afraid to challenge the status quo. She is able to train and influence teams in the Scrum methodology leading to self-enabled and self-delivering teams.*
>
> **-- Alisha Lee, Agile Coach**

> *Passion, Creativity and Goal Oriented are the words that come to mind when I think about Daria. She also has a very unique talent of finding creative solutions to solve problems whether its visual facilitation or through simulation games that she contributes with to the overall Agile community.*
>
> **-- Kajany Varatharajah, Certified Scrum Professional**

Made in the USA
Middletown, DE
12 March 2019